ATTRACTIVE DELUSION

Why a herd of individualists are walking of a cliff of climate change and migration

Gavin Cook

Copyright © 2018 Gavin Cook

All rights reserved.

ISBN-13:9781980564768

I don't know if ethical philosophy will allow itself to be called a social science, but when it mingles with moral psychology, it certainly brings out things which should not be missed when looking into cultural, unconscious decisions which play a large part in the direction of the entire planet.

.

CONTENTS

	Acknowledgments	I
	Introduction	1
1	Situation	17
2	Alternative Remedy	31
3	Identity and Individualism	45
4	Usual Responses	59
5	Power of the Herd	81
6	Personal versus Social Responsibility	99
7	Paradigm Maintenance or Paradigm Shift	118
8	State of the World	133

ACKNOWLEDGMENTS

Inspiration comes from the good and the bad. You can't beat a stick in the mud, who refuses, despite any holocaust of information, to accept that we are all in the shit. But then, you meet a seafarer, who's eyes have gazed at tranquility steeped horizons, and horror in the guts of a raging storm - and they just nod at you – which makes your whole week feel as if your own struggle is just a bit of toil you should take on the chin.

Attractive delusion

grumpy old man with a grip on the means of propulsion

INTRODUCTION

We are in a paradigm in western society, where individuals are seen as free to make what they can of themselves, in a system, which reflects the efforts and skills they put into this network. This brings about prosperity in the economy, as efficiency and competition provide the things desired by each other at the greatest speed. This is the *modus operandi* in general. Our collective wishes and desires are provided by each other, for a mutual gain from competitive interaction governed by the market mechanisms. This can also be seen as a global phenomenon, international trade doing the same thing. In the western world, over the last few decades, we have come to embrace the general principles of the free-market, and the liberty of the individual to generate their own well-being, through interaction and activity. This removes the hindrance of unnecessary organizational interference from a ruling body. Activities are given credibility on their own effectiveness in meeting the desires of those wishing to benefit from their provision. The guidance system for this engine is mostly the self-interest of the individuals participating, which collectively brings about the greatest good for those involved. This contributes to the psychological platform of individualism, leaning toward a greater emphasis on personal character and traits over situational circumstance, or collective mutual progression. We do things and buy and sell things. With effort and skill, we may earn enough money to buy the goods and services we want. The ideas of shopping, or working, are not unfamiliar. Neither is the concept of the free-market. But the way these simple principles interact to make the ideology of individualism, which is a psychological tilt, not a mechanical operating system to guide efficiency, has unexpected outcomes.

Many glitches may well pass through the net of this operating system. On the whole these can be counteracted by a governing body, legislating in different ways, to discourage those things seen as not representing the goal of this collective society. For example, taxation on tobacco, and the changes to smoking in publicly occupied spaces, has made improvements to the health of the nation through discouragement. The topic of interest to this book is the production of pollution and its' consequence of a warming planet, most often nowadays referred to as 'climate change'. This, is a disruptive change to the planets temperature, bringing about mostly long-term negative side-effects, which is definitely not being dealt with in the format that other undesirable phenomena are.

Instability on its' own may bring difficulties. For example, agricultural habits of different countries have hundreds of years of cultural history. These methods and systems, including the choice of which species of crop or cattle, are enveloped within social constructs. A hefty and swift shift in weather patterns, can give this normality a shake-up that is hard to deal with. Traditions and local knowledge have to be jettisoned. Stability, hundreds of years later may arrive, but on a planetary level, this will make some regions less suitable for providing food, and others more suitable. Not only would this require a shift in food types, but would also create a large shift in where people are, or an increase in death from starvation. Death and migration are currently, and to a greater deal going to be, occurring as a consequence of the amount of pollution being created by the activities of people, leading to changes in the planets climate. Some of those activities are happening now, some before now, and with great certainty some about to happen. This, it should be clear, is not a desirable outcome, and can only be seen as not in the interests of any collective society. After the climate summit in Paris, the subject of climate change has finally joined other subjects in the categories of 'things, which are part of reality'. There's still room for a bit of doubt and flexibility in interpretation, but, there has been a global agreement on the issue, describing outcomes in terms of upward changes in degrees centigrade. This means the mutual turning point of understanding and acceptance has been reached. There is a divergence between those countries, which have up to now been the greatest causers of these outcomes, and those whom are at the harshest places of the after-effects, both now and in the future.

We have a relatively free-market, in principle enabling individuals to most effectively achieve their desires. In the resulting side-effect of pollution however, this is at the moment simultaneously bringing about forces, which will cause long-term suffering, not seen as desirable by anyone. The causes of a large proportion of this impact, is the consumption of things chosen by consumers, not forced upon themselves by government action, but the simple wish to have or do something, most of which are a request for something to be done which will invoke, often unwarily, the production of pollution. We have had well over twenty years to take the issue seriously and find methods for resolving these difficulties, which are available. But, it is worth noticing that this collection of nations seem to be worsening the problem, on a consistent trend of increasing pollution. The best so far is to decrease the rate of increase. This doesn't mean we have the need to stop eating food or living in houses with cars parked outside. The element missing from curtailing the unnecessary occurrence of death and destruction, appears to be a lack of conscious application of effort to sort out the problem. At the same time the inevitable result, not desired by anyone, is becoming more certain. How does this come about? It turns out the answers lie in personal and sociological psychology. The way we make decisions and frame our thinking, is affected by our collective social mindset, as well as political and economic norms. This is the process, through which, we come to the disparity of having a freedom to choose what we wish for, and mostly unconsciously, being complicit in the manufacture of a disharmonious future with foreseeable and avoidable societal suffering. This sometimes can be called a 'tragedy of the commons'. We have a huge number of choices every day, without centralised administrative control, leaving us free to express our wishes in our actions and the goods and services we pay for. But somehow, the normality behind virtually all the things on the menu, is to continue on the path set by the rest of us, which will, as it happens, lead to social and economic global instability, brought about by food supply difficulties and mass migration. The chain of events bringing us those things, usually leads to a production process and the use of a product that will cause pollution. As it turns out, there can be consumer-based decision making, without blinkering out pollution-based side effects. The idea of being healthy and happy in a considerate lifestyle, which allows some of the complications to simple wishes, should not be thought of as contradictory to a modern successful western world. Efficiency in many variables can provide the same things with a reduction in the unwanted side effects. Pleasure can be delivered in a different way. The perception of this whole area being taken as an unwanted frustration to the normal pattern of life, comes from the existence of the simple paradigm of beneficial consumerism; which is hosted by society in general, as a collective mindset, which pervades the core directive for most of our activities. The motivational driver we live with, is not geared to take on any result-effecting modifications. The consequences of this inflexibility, will however lead to unnecessary suffering. This is a simple reflection on the current trajectory of the state of the world - the psychology of the 'self-interested individual' providing the collective benefits, is not co-joined to the additional principle of investigating or being concerned about the side-effects that brings about unwanted consequences. The propulsion of a weighty machine which refuses to acknowledge the harm it is bringing on to its' own long-term self, needs monitoring. If this is what is happening, is this well known? This phenomenon is very rarely acknowledged.

It turns out most people are quite content to be part of this self-destructive momentum. If an observation of this causal connection is made, it is responded to in a number of psychological patterns. Being in no control of the direction of the tide one is part of and can't influence, is often accompanied with a kind of quiet grin, which loves the benefits we believe we are reaping from this collective pathway, whilst not having the ability to be seen as having any responsibility for this. There is a comfort to a heaspace which believes that you are being handed some of the bounty, with or without making any decisions. It alternatively, can be that the difficulties facing us are understood, but not brought out to avoid the discomfort it would bring to show awareness of this negative aspect of our current trajectory. Sometimes however it is not allowed this credibility, which causes the making and maintenance of, different levels of delusion or distraction, which need maintaining to keep the basic mental pictures of aspirations and surroundings uninterrupted. Something which is simple to understand, the building blocks of cause and effect, are kept away by a tanglement of understanding, the success of which is kept going due to the attractiveness of the inner motto. 'Greed is good - self-interest is followed to help everyone as well as yourself - getting what you want is what makes things work.' This motivational paradigm is a way of letting yourself of many hooks, but cannot be worn at the same time as acknowledging that you are happy to create unnecessary damage. Paradigm maintenance requires this unexpected interference coming from reality, to be shoved off to one side. The reason this doesn't usually get noticed, or not consciously taken into consideration, is due to the effectiveness of this generalized character format which is taken on by society as a whole, and gives this trait resilience. A big part of this character forming, is in the shape of individualism. At the same time as the societal goal can be headed for by following self-interest in the market, the modern, personal viewpoint is to consider the individual as the building block of identity and achievement. This is not an historical consistent. Over past decades, motivational drivers have been in totally different ballparks. The attributes of reserve and prudence, where seen as admirable. Other characteristics such as honour, duty or integrity, quite often accompanying religious belief systems, have previously been the core direction of aspiration. Self-interest is usually around somewhere, but not usually at the front. I am purely making an observation of the diversity of alternatives, not giving a recommendation of what outlooks on life may be preferable. Compared to these possibilities though, it should not be surprising that a new kind of freedom focused on seeking to fulfill ones own desires as a priority, in a market system designed to encourage belief in this as being interaction in a way which benefits everyone, is a leap of faith that once taken by the whole of society, is resistant to change. Self-interest is a simple cog, to be given respect as a driver behind an economic principle. This is brilliantly compatible though, with the psychological principle of individualism, determining the scale of units of identity. The desirability of this simple focus on your self, naturally makes there a distance between your own activities and the wide world of consequences, as a result of narrowing the field of vision to personal desires. Time, effort and concentration are used up in making your best, personal, hallmark stamp on the canvas of yourself, perceived by your surrounding society. If reality inhibits this activity, it is told to go away. It should therefore be of no surprise that being made aware of this psychological feedback loop, which is causing planetary damage, is usually unwelcome. If it is this inhibition which happens to be taking the world down with it, this tough nut needs to be cracked, as 'understanding' is the key to most futures which are not blunders.

The world is changing fast, and most of us seem to be asleep in terms of how we are making some of this happen, and doing so unnecessarily. Is it just not very fashionable to care? It certainly is not best for everyone that we continue on the same path, convinced by our own delusions. Where does this aspiration to remain misguided come from, is it cultural, or are oligarchs pulling the strings? The good news is that there can be change, and that doesn't mean having a frugal existence being suppressed by misery. The purpose of this book, is not to prescribe possible remedies, just to uncover what is going on now, and why. The future is open, hopefully with people understanding the state of the planet with a rational understanding and an effective morality, not delusions and herd-like inconsiderateness.

The subject is an investigation into the interface between cultural identity and our ability to respond to the phenomenon of climate change. It is, part moral, part social psychology, in how we process circumstantial evidence with differing interpretations, applying unconscious twists and societal influence. It is hard not to be drawn into the negative outcomes of what is in the environmental field. But this work is hopefully as inspiring as it is enlightening in the social psychology of how the ideology of modern, westernized individuals is not culturally fixed, and therefore more of an open book. The worlds' climate is changing, and yet, perhaps a little less so in the last few years, is not acknowledged as being real by a large proportion of society. The reasons for this are not scientific, they are psychological, and come from both personal and cultural levels, in where, and in what systems, we believe our aspirations are involved with.

How we frame our understanding, particularly as individualists in a consumerist society, has feedback on the effort we mentally put into notions such as morality and collective responsibility. In a behaviourist manner, a lot of reflection on the trajectory of society, is usually based on its' compatibility with the *modus operandi* already adopted. Unintended outcomes are inevitable, the interesting point being on how we might expect the mindsets of people to respond to changes in the world, which are relevant to this viewpoint.

With no attempt to be controversial, the salient features of the subject can be quite provoking, including migration and food security. Fortunately, dissecting this philosophically couldn't, in theory, be more impartial. If asked in one sentence – consumerist individualism has made morality psychologically go to sleep, so the western ideology is shooting itself and everyone else, in the foot.

The first chapter 'Situation' outlines how personal consumer decisions, governmental and corporate plans, bring about the consequences of pollution in the cause and effect process. Making a connection between consumerist desires and droughts in other continents can be complex, but the basic principles of what cogs in what machine are making the world go in the direction it is, is easy enough. I have tried to describe some of this in a brief manner, without equating numbers or making elaborate descriptions of doom. This part could be more specific and detailed, but there are plenty of publications and information platforms clarifying and giving factual information on this subject in the very wide, mixed and diverse area. The second chapter 'Alternative remedy' brings in the concept that caring about pollution doesn't mean that freedom of choice has to be jettisoned, or that happiness is no longer in the ballpark. Using creativity and consideration can keep life enjoyable, just not in the same way as seeking desire and success without caring about the unintended side-effects of productive processes. These thoughts are quite simple and factual, and these two chapters are quite short, before moving into a more philosophical field.

Chapter 3, 'Identity and Individualism', starts looking at self-identity in how, even though this is about as personal as you can get, the format for this perception, is moulded by the society this is made from within. In a consumerist, individualist culture, the concepts of collective identity are still there, but not very prominent, as responsibility of success and achievement, are held up as signifiers of the individual. Motivations and aspirations focus on a close-to-self field of vision. This highlights the suitability of adopting this particular frame of self-assessment in a consumerist, free-market economic environment focused on individual desires.

When the climate issue is brought up, this normally triggers a range of responses, which are best described, not as a rational analysis of circumstantial evidence, but subconscious, emotional self-maintenance programs. Chapter 4, 'Usual responses', opens up a great can of worms with examples, which, I hope may clarify these various strategies of expressing beliefs on the subject. We all know we have some responsibility, and produce some pollution (carbon emissions), so any comment on this subject stirs a feeling of blame or involvement, which needs dealing with in some way. Making climate change not exist as part of reality is one method, which is factually wrong, but psychologically very simple. This is not to forget that there is nothing wrong with not wanting it to be real, as it is bad news without a lot of winners anywhere. Along with this simplistic method of keeping the mental slate clean for business as usual, other ways of coping with the subject of climate change, are clarified. This is not to dismiss or criticise these differing views, but as much to reveal where the motivations and triggers for these come from, explaining how, they should be expected, given how we are and what the situation is. However, a lot of these diversionary tactics have the opposite effect of leaving the mind open to change when evidence is pointing in that direction. This includes differences in how far from the self we allow our concern to stretch, both in terms of space and time.

Chapter 5, 'The power of the herd' is about the free-market and our trust in the invisible hand with its' ability to deliver the best for everyone. Voting with our feet, consumer decisions keep the pathway working. The concept of environmental concern however, comes along as an interruption. Having an unconscious awareness that this additional variable may have a restrictive affect on our liberty, we often prefer to stick with the majority rule, having things go the way they already do, on mass. Decisions over whether I want something or not, is in an area demarcated as separate from any ethical subject. A significant reason for this, is it's being available to me or anyone else there in the market place, as an indication of acceptability. This is not a one size fits all analogy, but is the general state of play. This chapter looks at the diverse ranges of consumer decisions in how some have more scope for variance than others. But most of all, it highlights how we cherish our liberties to an extent, that some subjects are dealt with by not allowing our pattern of aspiration to be interrupted, thereby reducing any further deliberation.

Chapter 6, 'Social versus Personal Responsibility', looks at how the ideology of consumerist individualism is a cultural perspective, which has a natural after-effect of reducing awareness to a limited priority area of personal desire. In having our self-identity being defined with a very limited connection to the effect we have beyond our own boundaries, our mental faculties are guided into a simple operating system that does not require a lot of thought in the field of collective responsibility. The psychological framework with which our surrounding society has helped us to construct and define the factors and variables which work together to attain success, and define our aspirations, streamline our thinking in ways which do not necessarily reflect the way things are without bias. This system contains rules of thumb as to when we do or do not bring in any consideration or feeling of responsibility. In such a way, many thoughts are absorbed by a way of consensus, and reflect where that culture is at that time.

Chapter 7, 'Paradigm Maintenance or Paradigm Shifts', discusses how difficult some changes in mind-set are, due to their very nature being a paradigm shift, in comparison to an update of an existing operating mode. In many ways, the ideology of consumerist individualism has been a great leap forward, liberating us from class restrictions, and reducing the desire for any regulations. The question is, can this framework of thinking adapt to a reality, which has harsh cause and effect feedback loops, these crossing national and generational boundaries. When self-esteem and personal identity have been guided by certain goalposts, the question is, is it more likely that the culture will show its' ability to frame things in a way compatible with keeping things set in that way, or make significant alterations? In terms of changes, we can look into how some shifts are harder than others. This includes how the surroundings in the modern age make the distribution of information faster than ever, making evidence-based global understanding more feasible, whilst not making aspirations or consumerist desires any different.

Chapter 8, 'The state of the world', is more forward looking than the previous more descriptive sections. Given the state of play, we can see some views becoming less credible as reality unfolds. This doesn't mean people of this mindset will change, but will have an effect on the melting pot of cultural outlook. General knowledge on the subject of global temperatures and the movement of people around the world, is a baseline future ideologies have to fit themselves around. These can take different directions, including emphasising national identity in order to tighten borders. The concepts of responsibility and individualism will struggle to find a coherent pattern to form around the disparity of well-being based on globally location-fixed opportunities. The strings that do the pulling to get things into this situation are psychological. If a culture generates a belief that blame is always to be directed outward, then a switch to any form of responsibility is hard. The consumerist, individualist ideology does though have an adaptable pattern of belief formation, if the goals need to move. This is how aspirations and the general perceived direction of progress are defined on mass by our cultural paradigms and how they form our field of vision. As a concluding chapter, which is a 'this or that direction' description of possibilities and probable outcomes, it is I hope, insightful and readable about an undetermined future.

Attractive delusion

Attractive delusion

SITUATION

The questions needed to be asked, are in relation to westernized individualistic society, and how its' activity is related to climate change and migration, and in what ways are these variable. A good starting point is to look at the direction we are heading in and what activities are bringing this about. Increased migration is, along with other things, one of the after effects of a warming planet. Due to forms of cultural and agricultural instability from a changing climate, people become displaced by food and water shortages, or by conflict over related resources, which may have previously not been so scarce. This is a simple sequence of variables, of pollution leading to a warmer planet, this then becoming less hospitable in some areas, and this leading to the movement of people away from these areas. Without there being barriers to prevent the movement of these people, it is with certainty that we can forecast that this is the future which lies ahead. As we are already on an irreversible two degree warmer planet trajectory, the concept of people everywhere remaining in their fixed locations is ridiculous. Less related to international migration, but still making people displaced, is the increase in coastal areas, which are highly populated, being flooded due to sea level changes. This is in addition to flash flooding from weather patterns, which can have diverse consequences in different geographical regions. The planet is warming in a time faster than can be adapted to easily. This will probably continue on its' upward trend after its' severity becomes undeniable, and will be very disruptive and bring suffering. There is chance of the well-being of people around the world being maintained by a sustainability strategy of adaptation and assistance, supporting changing landscapes and health needs. With this tiny bit of hope being a lot less likely than increased doom, it is best to look at the more probable difficulties of starvation, migration and conflict. Why are the causes of a lot of this future not comprehend by most of us, as being brought about by us in the 'developed west' in any reversible way?

The modern idea of individualism in the West is very much joined to the idea of consumer based free-market activity. One could express oneself in a communist country, but the sense of identity is very much more, at least in theory, linked to a concept of state or nation of governance, rather than being at liberty to express yourself in the things you buy, and how you got to being able to afford them. Rather than representing a collective identity formed in a concept of co-operation, the thing by which to make judgments in the consumerist West, is by me for myself, in complete independence of other people. All activities usually have some connection with pollution, but consumer based decisions, as opposed to activities not including purchases or transactions, have a very tangible sequence of personal psychological choices and their effects.

When looking into the connection between consumer activity and pollution, it is worth briefly looking into how this fits into the whole schema. The magnitude of the pollution created is the issue, meaning some things may have less significance than others. Military action abroad brings with it pollution as a side effect. Building motorways or ring roads, also cause pollution, which are not directly but are indirectly connected with consumer activity. Society as a whole, does carry the responsibility of the consequences of these things, and in some ways the desires of some members of society, including government, are connected to these undertakings, including the choice of light bulbs used in a hospital. But it is clear that we don't usually have much of a say in these things, but as an individual in the country doing these things, these can be considered as part of the baseline of the pollution we all create. The psychology of these decisions is very different to the personal choices we make as consumers. The extent to which these different processes are changing things in the world, can be compared by working out the percentages of national carbon dioxide emissions they cause in comparison to other things. Some figures are available which describe per-capita emissions for different countries, worked out as an average given the populations, which can then be cross-referenced with the general categorisation of main pollution causes. Public concern is quite often voiced about energy supply from different power stations. This is an obvious natural attention dragger, given big chimneys or nuclear reactors. As a great area with potential for conversion to renewable energy, it also functions as a distraction from the less noticeable side effects from normal consumer based behaviors. The same is true for transport, which is a significant cause of pollution, also being easier to picture mentally than other things as we can hear the engines and see the fuel going in. Loads of consumer goods are wrapped in plastic packaging, with much more thinking needed to put together the connection between petrol-chemical manufacture, oil extraction, waste management, transportation etc. Food production and the distance it has traveled, is also very important. This brings emotional responses, as we all have an intuitive connection to the stability of our needs and enjoyment of not being hungry. We can see the causes of pollution are diverse and some more complicated than others. A simple fact though, is that in the consumerist West, we pollute more per person than many other places in the world. In some countries, it is needed to factor in their surrounding ambient temperatures, as in Baltic countries for example, the need for energy use in heating is larger than in other areas. The same could be said to be true for air conditioning in hot countries, but not without noticing that many countries are very hot and not known for refrigerating the air around themselves.

The simple correlation between wealth and production of pollution is roughly true. Along with this is the analysis of wasteful consumption. Wealthy countries, to a large extent having had the benefits of the industrial revolution before other nations, are a simple majority of having created the problem of climate change. The proportion of current emissions between the historically developed and what can be called the new 'emerging economies', is changing. This means there is a balance sheet of those previously responsible, and those now making things worse. What this book is trying to reveal, is how concepts such as resolution, fair-play, considerateness in a bright future, have been washed away by the psychology of the individualist consumer.

The mixture of things causing pollution varies in complexity of 'cause to effect' factors. They also vary in how easily they are seen to be connected with the choices of the individualist consumer. Government policy changes, and decisions made at the corporate level, show little resemblance to the triggers of desire made by the people in the shops. As a culture though, we show our general ethos. There is a whole spectrum of differing beliefs within a society, but the main thrust of the culture can be identified. How much of this is a consequent of the masses choices, versus top-down rule, is a major hinge of that society. Not all of the effectiveness of this divergence of influence comes from direct physical influence. As a culture we define acceptable and unacceptable paths. A lot of this can be in consumer decisions, with legislation having to keep within the parameters of these things remaining available. Having an interconnected care for the entire planet, is possible as a form of identity in an individualist consumer society, but this frame of mind is in ways the opposite of what is a more embedded pattern of development of focusing on ones' self in a liberated market place. As a culture which has materialistically benefited hugely from its' trek down this path, the rubber stamp of its' mindset is not an ethical outreach, more an inward looking cost-benefit reward system of having or doing things.

To describe the nature of what is happening to the world and where this is being caused, the perpetrator is carbon emissions, which can be worked out as carbon equivalents to include other greenhouse gases caused by the activity, which have more or less effect than carbon dioxide. For over twenty years the subject of climate change, or global warming, and pollution, have been in the open as a significant, but not necessarily the most important issue of the time. What hasn't happened though, as a society, is any scale of learning which could be called 'carbon literacy'. If I was to compare the benefit caused by you changing your central heating system with my changing the make of my car, we could discuss the tons of carbon per year, versus embodied energy in manufacture, with an open mind. However, if I mention approximately how many tons is created by someone's seat on a return flight to Spain, more often than not, this will not appear to be in an understandable language, nor of any interest to the individual. This shows that in general, we are not connected with the issue enough to be able to compare the magnitude of different activities. This would enable choices to be made that would make a difference. One thing may be easier to do than another and reduce my emissions by a lot more, but on the whole, people aren't interested, and are not carbon literate. This signifies that attention on how best to solve the problem, has not been present in our society, for a long time. As a culture, we in the West have spent over two decades making the issue twirl around or go away, using other methodologies rather than looking at the causes in our own activities and consumption.

The phenomenon here we are trying to get a clarifying understanding of, is global. This is both in its' cause and its' effect. The Arctic is heating up quicker than the rest of the planet, but things are changing everywhere. The effects of a warmer planet are diverse, global, and not usually beneficial. The direction we are heading in, is in a literal translation, only available as a forecast. This is not by choice, as, if I predict the sun will rise tomorrow, this too is a forecast. The trustworthiness of this could be called into question. Scientifically things on this matter are quite clear, not without variables, but the ball-parks of pre-industrial revolution era and the warmer world we are moving into, are very much distinct. The climate debate has been very messy. But that is a debate. It does become apparent, particularly recently when the science and evidence is clearer, that a large amount of this is psychological in terms of our mental ability to accept that things are changing. In terms of bringing to the table a reasonable outline of the future, which by definition is a forecast, can still be done. There is a large amount of literature covering this doom-laden but regrettably real perspective. Without avoiding depressing information by skirting around reality, what we can do is try to keep this short. A technique for this can also be vagueness. One degree rise (over the 1961 to 1990 average), was previously at climate talks discussed as to be avoided if Africa and other sensitive areas were to be kept on a safe path. This is now not even feasible, as we're at about 0.84 already, way ahead of any 2020 or 2050 target talk. Two degrees rise is a new target, which will lead to many parts of the world becoming very different at an incredibly fast rate of change compared to other geological shifts. This target is however, not in the bag in terms of probability. Given the path of emissions and the difficulties in turning this about, we have shown a lack of ability in not having not done so thus far. Which therefore brings us into what things, albeit in a variable manner, we can expect to see in the future.

Which parts of the world will get how much warmer and when, and how this will effect the landscape is an important and interesting subject. Two degrees is a big shift. People could map out their own countries to define what changes could be expected in what time scales. One factor which has come to attention in the western world as well as other regions, is the risk of potential flooding. How many homes and workplaces will become unusable, or at least uninsurable, is a variable of global importance. Many highly populated areas are in coastal locations around the world, due to the historic and current activities of shipping and fishing. The ability of highly developed cities to survive changes in sea level, is in part down to their willingness to fund additional flood defences. Here we have the combination of weather patterns with a nations' wealth, creating different types of difficulty compared to the 'most at risk' as referred to by some NGO's. These difficulties in densely packed areas are very different to the means of coping with sudden changes in rural flash flooding, in areas more connected with subsistence farming than city dwelling. Reports such as those by the UK climate change and migration coalition, clarify what variables effect different situations and locations.

Changes in weather patterns are going to cause changes in what crops and cattle can be farmed where. The Sahel region of Africa has for some time been sensitive to these changes, which will increase. Spain, California and parts of Australia have droughts, which will not abate. The list and the analysis can go on. Water shortages is a large and internationally important subject. The global climate conferences are, without making things clear, a debate on who is going to suffer, where, when, and who cares enough and understands enough now to try to manage their countries responsibility for bringing this about, combined with what particularly in America, seem to be relatively non-binding agreements on emissions reduction in the future. Clarity for everyone to understand would be great. The collective outcome has a global consequence, which unfortunately, does need to be spelled out. The idea of explaining to people that we would like to help them out, but as things have already gone a bit far, they're going to have to leave their countries and find somewhere else to live, sounds like something that could not happen without either hysterics or outrage. This however, is exactly what is already being revealed to the small island states under the unstoppable path of sea level in the short-term climate adjustment.

Here's an interesting point though. There's not going to be an ice age. There should be one about now. After an interglacial period of twenty thousand years, due to the earths' wobble on its' axis, with a subtle combining effect of the earths spinning around the sun in a non-perfect ellipse, the planet goes back in to a chilling period of about one hundred thousand years, and then there is another interglacial period. The rate of warming as a result of burning fossils, which come from a carbon sequestration over fifty million years, used in a period of about one hundred and fifty years, has overridden this normal phenomenon. I have been a bit sketchy and dramatic, but the point I'm making is actually in the opposite direction. If environmentalists are to be seen as nature lovers who protest at the interruption of natures' path of succession, then we should be regretting the bypass of an ice age. With a simple look at the expected extinction of species and huge suffering to humans from trying to adapt to such a phenomenal shift into ecosystems on an icy planet, we can see the wonderful plethora of life that surrounds us now, despite the ignorant and inconsiderate treatment of it by ourselves, is in part an accidental foothold. Let's not let that be a 'so far so good' though, because things are moving very fast and powerfully enough to shift things in a not very good direction. A bit of a positive reflection on the beauty of our current surroundings, despite our daftness, can be a helpful break from looking at the difficulties we seem to be showing at making steps forward without blasting ourselves backwards.

Just to emphasize the confusing polarity of our psychological state, which is in a large part responsible for the lack of a coherent response to the existing dilemma, are two examples of what are being discussed at the moment. There has been press on how in terms of global welfare, the changes are on an irreversible path, covering how food security over a fifty year period will have made the transition to very difficult times, as transportation over large distances will be difficult, and how productivity becomes scattered and different. In this way there will be no available path to make things resemble the good times we have now, with the huge varieties and great availability we have on the global menu. At the same time is a persistent discussion of how mechanized robots will take over the need to do as much work and definitely remove the need to drive cars, leaving us in a quandary of how to define purpose, status and reward in a comparably inactive state.

When broken down into the necessary ideas that constitute these ideas, they are completely counter-posed. Food insecurity means we need to devote some time and effort into correcting the path of our activities to remedy the situation and bring about a reasonable existence without hunger and despair. The arrival of the shortages to large numbers of people means problems have occurred and more attention needs to go into these areas. Having a robot deliver your pizza, means you have had such a surplus of material and effort, and have such a productive chain of events behind you, the only concerning feature left in your existence is the need to somehow develop a sense of meaningfulness in your otherwise placid consumerist state. One discussion is that things are going so bad they are on a downward spiral that will not change. The other discussion is a fear that things are going so well for us in how we develop our technical productivity, that everything is going to come to us so easily we need to work out how to strategize this functional ease. Both of these ideas are centred on forecasts of adaptation. However, for both of these to happen at the same time, means there has to be a very definitive distinction between those who suffer, or are going to, and those who think that things are advancing in ways which need less connection with humans collectively producing things. There can be social divides in either of these scenarios. The owners of the automated world have a great advantage over those in their society who remain without status and have a reduced chance of active employment. Scarce food supply also doesn't mean everyone is going to go without in the same way. The starting point of the automated world though, definitely doesn't come from the world of scarcity. What it increases is productivity without human input. The development of this requires resources and investment from somewhere. These are high-end mechanistic materials and significant financial ability, being motivated by the desire of it being worthwhile in the predicted outcome, to the provider of this innovation. This, without even digging for a rationale, is not in the direction of reducing the likeliness of there being a global instability of food resources, it is from the mindset of those who believe their resources are secure and wish to reconfigure how they are processed and delivered. These two subjects are not related at all in their speculation, but they clearly show how our cultural identity is open to a large range of dispositions to the future, some of which are incompatible with each other.

One of the reasons there is vulnerability to inconsistency in any speculation, is that science and political debate are in their very nature dislocated from each other. This is rightly so, as socio-economic prevarication is not a matter of measuring and understanding. Elements of aspiration and ideology are about how to mould the future based on a vision. This is in part how we translate where we think we are at in this time, and in part a creative forward looking view at both how things could, and given our trajectory, will, end up later on.

Attractive delusion

Attractive delusion

Attractive delusion

ALTERNATIVE REMEDY

Just in the way that alternative remedies may have a status of being seen by most as being a bit off-field, so does the idea that western idealism can have a modification. The idea of making changes which would provide solutions to excess pollution is normally met with dismay. This is not to say that red tape is to be added to everything. What is it about the normal mindset that feels that the current framework for thinking is set in stone and not available for analysis or judgment? The idea that the free market, left to its' own devices can put things into motion which cause unnecessary harm, should bring a response of some sort of appeal for investigation, intervention or change. This new tack does not definitely mean that people would thereby loose their freedom to choose which things they want. Nor would this necessarily be inconsistent with wealth distribution patterns being governed by other factors. It also doesn't mean that those who choose things which cause the least pollution, should be seen as forsaking their own desires, like fasting or wearing a hair shirt. In a society that sees how consequentially, some things are fun, desirable, whilst at the same time being undamaging, could make some things a goal and not a restriction. All this means is that as well as wanting or not wanting something, as well as being able to afford it, a small amount of consideration needs to be done about the possible side effects of this choice, which may not effect directly how enjoyable this thing is to yourself. Or, if this is an impediment to those simply observing or instinctively doing something, they can if they choose just ignore the possible damage caused by things now and then.

This however, does not resemble the value system adhered to by most western societies. Freedom to choose which goods and services are desirable to the consumer, is a functional programme. Along side of this though, is the goal-driven motivator of how to measure the relative success and status of individuals through wealth, not only in a security of assets behind closed doors, but material displays of ability to purchase. The requirement of any attempt to limit the damage caused by accidental warming of the planet, is to reduce pollution, mostly in its' creation. Many symbols of success in western consumerist societies, bring about the side effect of making those people pollute more than other people. Larger cars, with the ability to cross mountains, as well as carry people, due to weight and size, need larger amounts of fuel. But as well as causing, by most of their users, unnecessarily increased pollution, these machines are actually a symbol of success, brought about by the cost of manufacturing bigger and better 'stuff' than others, making them expensive to purchase and run – thus, a display of wealth. Here we are in a society of individuals, these people having independence to express their desires and ability to get them. At the same time as government leaders from all around the world discuss the problems created by pollution, the aspirations of a lot of people from the cultures they represent, is to cause a completely unnecessary amount as a badge of honour and as an acquisition to be proud of.

The same applies to the jet-set. Those people who are wealthy enough to travel the world at a whim, are obviously in a great position. The factual reality of a cross-continental trip causing a huge amount of pollution per person, is not usually allowed in to the cost-benefit calculation in the praise or admiration for the producer of this. When you see aeroplanes fuelling up on runways it gives you a bit of an idea, otherwise it can be looked up in tons of carbon per person making that trip. Having the world as accessible as that, is great though, and naturally is desirable, for those who can. This rarely comes with any recognition of the amount of damage done to the atmosphere by these people compared to those who are unable to, or choose not to. Large houses without modern standards of insulation/energy efficiency are another sign of achievement. It's better to have a bit of history attached to a great 'pile'. So here is the contradiction, which pervades through society at the individual level, no matter how seriously one's government has taken the issue. We need to cause less pollution, but our motivational goals at this time, are not engineered to allow thoughts such a 'less is more', to enter our guidance system, as more of anything, apart form debt, is the general rhythm of the base line. Things cost money, and success is having lots of both. Having a lot of wealth and enjoying yourself, is an attractive position to be in. But accidental harm being brought about by this 'above normal' consumption, is a real consequence. Having prosperity, could alternatively, enable an individual to spend time and money, or someone else's time, on causing less pollution, whilst benefiting from the things they want to achieve or have. This does seem like an unlikely twist, as in our everyday subconscious mind-set, this is not consistent with the normal direction of our ambitions, which is designed to be unimpeded by any concern for the welfare of other things or individuals outside our own individualism. Success is a playground that does not want interruptions. 'Care free' is a great state of mind. This is usually only in a short-term moment though, in contrast to the normal balancing act of being mentally active in assessing the situation and your surroundings with foresight. If the concept of being carefree is persistent into a long-range personality realm, that means the agent has adopted into their character a paradigm that does not respond to circumstance.

The symbolism of success having very little compatibility with living a considerate lifestyle, has effects beyond its' own limited realm of existence. Our desires to achieve betterment of our times alive, have normally gained some of their goals by those who are already where we want to be. This is not to say we never have the ability to free-think, but that as a feature of being in a society, we absorb a lot of the collective motivations around us. This means that although poor people don't have the assets to produce an unnecessarily large amount of pollution, they wish they could, as anyone would, using the desirable avenues for gratuitous consumption put on display by the rich. Things can change, but the principle of changing a format of thinking is much harder if you're swimming against the majority stream. This is particularly true when the paradigm is considered to be normal and not manufactured by ourselves in any way, and not easily variable in any manner. This is true of the current predicament, as the herd of individualists have designated their own destiny through mass collusion, in a complicit majority rule which is very hard to not go along with.

If the cold, rational appraisal is put forward to individuals, of the unwanted side effects of pollution as a consumer, there are three main formats of response. The simplest, is that the judgmental input of possible damage caused by consumerist activity, is rejected. In other words, the disruptive factor of pollution is not accepted as an allowable element into the decision making process. An alternative, more calculated response, would be to involve this element into the choice making, or judgment process, which is what I suggest is the most appropriate, systematic resolution. Desire and aspiration are still there in the shop with you, but with a small amount of thought being allowed to co-join these. This however, normally leads to complications brought about by a dissonance with the consumerist normal procedure, causing this process to be rejected as a feasible ideology by most people. Freedom of the consumer, is subconsciously creating the efficiency of non-calculation, which would not like to be rectified. A third, more radical 'hippy' response, is to reject the initial format of 'more is good' in return for a 'less is better', 'small footprint' ideology, which is of course, incompatible with the normally assumed westernised consumerism. Because of the nature of this third way of response being seen as a groundbreaking, about turn response to the complication, the unappealing nature of the hippy alternative paradigm, creates an animosity to the interference of the consumerist strategy. This is understandable, as modifying the format of thinking from having what you want, to living from a completely different perspective, is a big shift. Even though the method of including a new considerate element is a lot less radical, this is also rarely accepted. So normally compromise, or modification to the normal *modus-operandi* of unabated consumerism, is not usually allowed and is consciously or unconsciously rejected.

What we are looking at, is how the nature of consumption responds to the new interruptive variable and what this means. At the heart of this is morality, as this new input very much has an 'oh dear' element to it. So the responses we see are the interaction of consumerist, or 'normal' desires, with the new question posited to investigate the acceptability of the outcomes brought about by these. This is very different from asking people for moral judgments on the matters of things which are neither caused or desired by the individual. General moral principles, for example on the potential threats of nuclear war, are debated in a constructive/deconstructive manner. As you can see, this is quite different from the issues of individualist identity in a consumerist society and its' feedback loops on any moral constraints. In this way the subject of this book is in the field of applied moral psychology, not a theoretical moral debate about a subject, which differs in that it could be brought out into the open without emotional triggers taking precedence.

    An interesting way to uncover the distinct feature of the plateau of usual reactions, other than to dissect them under their normal frameworks, which will be looked at in other chapters, is to look at any hypothetical alternative, which can be contrasted with the currently more popular disposition. This can show what it is which is prevalent in the normal decision making, feasibility processes, and the elements which make this happen should become apparent.

    The quality of clothing is an interesting area. Having something that is made to last a long time, has long-term cost-benefits to the consumer. But short-term increase in manufacture requirements cause increases in purchase prices. Being a prudent, durability aware consumer, spending in a world of changeable fashion, is not a natural combination. In some designs with well-known labels though, this increased cost carries with it the status of desirability for that very reason. Resource use and pollution can be reduced, with credibility for the individual as an objectively successful attainment, but restricted in its' availability due to disposable income, not through any moral standards of constraint. In this case, polluting less, costs more, which is why for at least for some people, makes this product more appealing. This shows how the cogs do not always spin in different directions. The third cog in the middle of this synchronization of consumerism and environmentalism, in this area of our current social climate, is mostly a display of having plenty of spending money. This is not a respect for the integral quality of the fabric item and its' life-cycle analysis. However, if an object has desirability that happens to carry the aspects of a less wasteful consumption of clothing, this element may become more prominent in a sensible world. This has a positive aspect, as it shows we are not automatically drawn towards a more disposable, wasteful mindset. We rarely find the idea of cheap clothing desirable because it can be discarded at will. That idea carries with it the sense of it being not very good, which a lot of us still follow, down to necessity. The quality of it can send it to the bin quicker than we would like. Whether or not you have the money to buy quality goods is another matter, but at least the goal of this 'quality-desirability' causes a less damaging lifestyle, which is down to a want, not a constraint.

As expressed earlier, the idea of allowing in the new variable of contemplating the amount of pollution being caused, to be allowed in, is a consideration to be blended in with the other factors. This does not automatically dictate a new mantra of not liking fun or happiness. For example, if you are fortunate enough to own your own home, and have gone to the trouble and expense of installing an electrical-generating-photovoltaic solar system, there should be significant savings in the cost of living for yourself in the future. This cost reduction means other activities can be paid for, or perhaps less paid work done to get to the existing standard of living. Here there is a distinct absence of any 'oh dear' element. Calculations about the current subsidies, and the normal cost of buying energy generated by other means, obviously complicate this example, but here shows how individual choices, are very much in this case in the playing field of improving the collective existence of people on the planet, and are not necessarily at the same time chastising oneself of positive steps. I've worked myself on using an unusually large thermal water storage tank, to allow a thermal solar drain-back system to contribute to an underfloor-heating system as well as domestic hot water. This is not created by governmental legislation restricting my ability to turn my boiler on and pay my own bills. My ability to care about the planet and other people, has directed me into an area of engineering I would ordinarily not have had such an interest in. It is precisely this absence of negativity, which separates the example from the usual emotional responses of believing you are having consumerism redirected by new 'naughtiness' factors, with no positive sense of fulfilment in doing.

Going along with the more standard naughty elements, is in itself possible as a factor of deliberation that does not necessarily outlaw consumption. Waste is an issue in production processes, as well as in the life-cycle of the finished product. In clothing as well as other industries, recycleability is a variable which the consumer can be notified about, rather than being seen as not relevant. In the food industry, if you were aware that a lot of what you consume is being grown in unsustainable energy intensive greenhouses, you may have your enjoyment of it inhibited. Here we have a plethora of variables, relating to the wasteful sides of production, the life-cycle efficiency of the raw materials and other necessary aspects of the production and delivery processes. Some things have more diverse possibilities than others to make this an area of contemplation. You may like a process of adaptation to circumstance, rather than a constraint on the ability to have and do things.

There is a contrast here between the feasibility of positive responses and doom laden, restrictive practices. This is very much a sense of direction. If something is desired, and then a new variable comes along and complicates the flow of this pursuit, that is an interruption, particularly if this is a hindrance coming from a plateau of high moral ground. The worst cases of this, would be if the moral consideration is a complete antithesis to the desirable activity. In contrast to this are sometimes more tolerable bolt-on sustainability badges, which are acceptable tweaks, rather than an attempt to derail the honour of the direction of the desire itself. This is not to say that any of this is a desirable path of progress, just that these phenomena are already out there, in front of us as a population of consumers. We can observe this quite simply, in that positive activities and restrictive interruptions have different reactions. But the more important analysis is that this format of response is usually active in people already. As a perfectly natural way of keeping decision-making and behaviour as simple as possible, the preference is for short, straight lines over collages of multi-level judgments. For this reason, modifications to judgment patterns are hard to accept when they add complexity, which is exactly what environmental consideration is. This happens when it is added to the normal zone of consumerist desire. On top of this is a further influence of this being either a positive or negative signalling aspect. The difference between uninterrupted consumer choices and more deliberative judgments, can be described as two different levels of thinking. The same thing happens when cognitive patterns change in overcoming inhibitions, or addictive behavior. This makes it understandable why people who can quite calmly and rationally show their ability to discuss moral issues about any subject, then show when the concept of modifying consumer desire is injected, more of a gut reaction of annoyance. The concept of there being two different levels of thinking, lends itself to the idea that creativity is one of the major facets which bring benefits through a positive, adaptive thoughts. This makes mental activity a provider of joy and not a burden.

The first option is to reject outright the possibility of planet-changing pollution being considered in our day to day activities. This is a reflex response, to which there are the two remaining strategies. One alternative, mentioned before, which is to modify consumerist idealism, would not be a frictionless path and would stir up some cognitive dissonance. The third tactic, is to completely reject the materialist agenda and focus more on succeeding in health, well-being and survival, whilst minimizing the need for things and the corresponding damage caused by yourself. This can be referred to as hippy, non-consumerist path. The above is a crude over-simplification of the spectrum of three differing paradigms. But the principles behind what divides these three dispositions is clear at this primary level. Not recognizing pollution as a variable that needs to be taken into consideration, is usually a 'leave this thinking space alone' strategy. This can involve an active mental decision to reject this as not being real, or at least to be ignored.

Another, but less commonly expressed belief, which removes head-clutter, is the idea that this freedom of choice needs to be maintained by any moral principles being dealt with by the powers that be, before the choices are presented to the individual. That would be a faith in legislation to eradicate that level of thinking from the consumerist platform. Either way, these frames of mind retain the liberty of the consumer, without the need for extended thinking being needed by the entrance of this new variable into the decision making process. Being left to do what you want is great. But in an attempt to put a positive slant on the alternative strategies, this is in faith in people to use their own minds to think considerately, when the blindfolds are taken off about the unfolding chain of events. That makes this slightly more complex thinking an exciting realm for discussion and creativity. To presume it is best to let everyone plod around in the dark, with 'care' being done somewhere else, is to underestimate the ability of normal people to be involved, desire and be active in a decent world.

The alternative frames of mind of involving consideration or being motivated by a 'less is more' view do both have an element of restraint compared to a 'no need to care' approach. The need to deliberate to some degree about the side-effects of meeting some desires is not an end-goal though. This is purely an interruption of the process, which may slow it down and complicate it, but the result after this may be more or may be less pleasurable to the individual. It certainly makes the wish to always choose what you want without any of this fuss seem very shallow. The 'less is more' paradigm, is however, very different, in that it is a shift in the core driver. If materialist, consumer based desires are turned off as a motivator, this makes for a very different perspective on modern life. This is not a modification of normal westernized activities, applying a new factor into the judgment zone, it is a complete about turn. However, in the subject area of climate change, the end-of-line effect of this is to reduce damage caused by unnecessary consumerism. This is the same as applying moral consideration into westernized consumerism. These two alternatives, are therefore, different operating systems having a similar consequence, the 'hippy' stance appearing to be more extreme on a sliding scale of commitment. They both differ from unimpeded consumerism in having some level of care, but with different personal agendas.

If there is a preference for consumer activity to have a space without these hindrances, this is possible through regulation. Not caring is different from not having to care. If there is an open discussion about legislation on particular phenomena, and laws are enforced to ensure that certain principles are adhered to, this can make thought on the subject unnecessary. This is to know in the back of your mind that this has been dealt with. This would hopefully be with a sense of clarity that something that matters is being responded to. I'm afraid, that's quite a bit of a different situation usually, to being told by consumerist packaging that something ethical is being done somewhere - 'green wash'.

The major divide between the differing practical applications is by either having explicit legislation, or by making independent consumerist decisions not inconsiderate. Both of these show themselves as being far from incomprehensible to most people. Life does not need to have the anchors slammed on, or misery deemed as compulsory, which is entirely different from the situation we are almost certainly heading for, which looks as though it will include a large amount of suffering. So what is it that makes the destination we are headed to, not recognised by a lot of people as being part of real life? Why have the simple, different strategies to remedy this likely outcome not come out to be seen as a debate required by common sense?

Attractive delusion

Attractive delusion

How did this guy ever learn how to restore a 1930's Francis Turbine to convert a water mill into a hydro-electric plant?

IDENTITY AND INDIVIDUALISM

Individualism, as it presents itself, is a mindset which has more focus on the individual rather than the collective. We are all individuals in some form of society. But this way of thinking which is more prevalent in westernized societies, also has interpretations of responsibility that goes with it. Success or failure can come to the surface through hard work, bad luck, innate ability, and financial or physical assistance or hindrance. The individualist approach to this, is to focus on the responsibility of this outcome being the 'doings' of the person, over and above any circumstantial inputs. Other frames of thinking, often referred to as being more common in the Far East, have a more collective paradigm of thought. Here situations and surrounding influences are assumed to have had a more significant input. We can see how identity and responsibility become tied together. In an individualist culture, we are quite prone to blaming ourselves for where we have got to. This is true despite the un-level-ness of our playing fields. This concept of effort and ability, giving everyone a chance, is also at the centre of the

American dream. This can however, be contrasted with the ideas of collective identity and responsibility. It is true that in different cultures, if you are born into a certain demarcated boundary of identity, that is often taken as a given, the circumstances that necessarily follow it are accepted and deemed as irreversible. Along with this unenviable level of discrimination, also comes a frame of thinking which is more prone to compassion. As circumstances are seen in a more effective way than in the individualistic ideology, a person in a bad situation can be seen as someone who has had a bad run of luck, not just someone who has screwed up. Both of these frames of thinking can be in very unfair societies, but in a less individualistic one, your current well-being is seen as not being entirely down to your own efforts, other factors taking some of the responsibility, including your identity being in part handed to you by being type-cast. In the individualistic collective, the connectedness of the well-being of the individual and their own effort, affects their identity to a large extent. This lack of extending empathy to circumstantial inputs in your own and other peoples' achievements, comes as a reflex response which is an implicit analysis. This does also have a side effect, which can have beneficial effects. By blaming yourself and restricting your attention to the effectiveness of your direct inputs into achieving your goals, better things are likely to be achieved. Along with this focusing of effort, self-doubt is a good catalyst to progress. Even though how things go have many factors, the westernized psychological framework of individualizing the connection between personal effort and achievement, brings with it a motivational pattern that is a great way of distilling attention and effort. To get things done or achieve targets, this is positive. However, if this is the only mental operator, there are bits of being human missing. This includes being happy in this state of current achievement deficit, which can come in all different kinds of different applications. The psychological phrase of 'attribution error', refers to how the disposition of the individual may be overstated in the interpretation by others. With the bias not balanced around circumstance as well, it often involves personal blame over happenstance. The opposite of this would be fatalism, where what happens is just the way things were going to go, without psychologically bringing in the effectiveness of personal input.

The way one labels oneself has to work to a format embedded in your surrounding society. How we have people interpret where we are in our lives, or even 'what' we are to them, in a collective or individualist culture, is in a format generally framed by that culture. This is not an objective one size fits all stereotype that fits all people in all situations - which is why most of this psychological interpretation of the display you are thought to be showing, is unconscious. It is also true that not only do we become interpreted differently now and then, but our recognition of ourselves also varies. Without having a mental condition of a split-personality, we can have multiple identities. At a football match, at a dinner party, and waiting for a bus with strangers, we may have different genres of our own identity. This shows itself in how our accents can take on unintended variations, in addition to a variety of manners, vocabulary and body language. In the modern age, this presentation now varies in what communication medium we are connecting to others with. Text-talk versus boss-to-employee conversation, not only has a different language, but comes from a different side of our persona, both of which we consider to be ourselves, even though, from an outsiders' perspective, there would be very little obvious connecting features to identify the person. We can be situationally relevant in our presentation, unaware of the flexibility in our own identity. We have a flexible presentation of what we think people will make of us, and how we can swing this about to suit ourselves in different encounters. Without knowing it, we are working according to principles and rules that we have absorbed from our surrounding society. We are all encoded with patterns of interpretation that would take a lot of internalized digging into to clarify in a rational, literal manner. This is an interesting irony, in that even in a culture whose form of identity is focused on the concept of each agent as an individual, the shaping of the result is in part made under a collective umbrella.

Many, very different factors are some times more central in our identity. Fashion is a good example of a way of expressing a form of identity, without using any communication other than the visual, which can have effects on many of the people one then passes by. This is a simple strategy, which could however be totally misinterpreted in a different culture, or in the wrong situation. Part of this communication is the display, the undertaking of the individual, and the other half is the interpretation, which generally is a relatively collective paradigm, but can differ in terms of the size of the group. This is true for virtually all ways of forming an occurrence of self-identity. The framework the individual fits this around, is defined by the individual in a form of a context, which is produced by their take on a collective perception. So we have a two-sided equation, developed by the individual. One part is made out of the presentation the individual has made, as the agent would picture the others' picture of themselves.

The processes of evaluation and interpretation are in the collective field, with the current trend in the west being from the individualistic perspective. This is not all encompassing, as when something such as a televised charity appeal happens, our mental framework can shift back to a more cohesive 'don't just think about yourself' format. This has features the modern perspective has to an extent suppressed. Aspects of the modern age sense of identity are quicker and more flexible than they were in earlier times. Smart phones and the internet, have made communication much more fervent in its' frequency, but more inconsistent in our self-evaluation. Imagine in times before the phone, your role in society would have been communicated a lot less, usually in verbal exchanges and simple visual presentation, in a relatively steady state, as what you were was pretty well fixed. This had the downsides of a hierarchy-based society of class and status, with identity being anchored with near permanence, which is now more fluid. The shifts we have made into a more flexible pattern of society, is in a very real sense liberating, our labels no longer being quite so fixed. The speed with which we bat things about though, has the additional effect of our not being as concerned with the 'long-term' as we used to be. When in an uncomplicated position, the path ahead appears a lot clearer. Changes may be made to steer this in the direction of a beneficial long-term goal, taking thought and action, including some trust or hope. A bit like planting a tree, these things are not in the bag, but the 'probable' progress is obvious. The modern mind doesn't lend itself to this kind of less immediate deliberation. The here and now are more of a preference to us than it used to be, particularly if the long-term includes possible uncertainty. In the role of an individual, in a sea of people all trying to show their signifiers of what they are, their self-identity is dependent on this quick and fickle performance-stage. We are a lot more fluid, although this gives us all kinds of opportunities that otherwise would not be there. This does come along with a fragility of identity that you wouldn't have had when you are permanently down-trodden, or if more fortunate, on a semi permanent pedestal in a patriarchal age. This variability makes us focus on the more definitive and accessible near to hand. We can embed ourselves in varied and multiple roles, some with less real, tangible credibility than others, including virtual reality. For this reason, we are not as likely to make long-term emotional investments in things. This is not because it is now any less possible to make commitments or sincere dedications, which some people do. But due to the surrounding situation of there being a bigger more varied plethora of identity displays and games, conscious and unconscious directional decisions are in a very wide field of vision which includes some very short-term pay-offs.

Identity is a lot of times a motivator. This calculation is made by the individual, where the collective mind-set is approximated, rightly or wrongly, and within this there is a goal they would like to achieve in themselves. This is a natural habit, as making up your own set of parameters and aspirations, with definitive variables, is not impossible, but would require in depth analysis and introspection in a very contemplative way; which is still possible, but less likely, given the efficiency of using a ready-made alternative. One may absorb the definitions of desires of most of society around you, with some involvement of personal preferences, but a large amount of it being an unconscious encoded guidance, with a box within it, we tick as desirable. Here, the goalposts of most of our lives, are given rough locations, with a certain amount of flexibility given different timing and situations. But in many ways this collective, unexpressed, definition of desire, is what makes up the language of our internal thoughts as to what is it we want to do in order to climb our own happiness ladder. How we see ourselves in terms of identity, comes from an impression others have on us from our theoretical rehearsal of how they would react to our goals, and the achievements we have made so far. This is not to say we have no introspective contemplation times, but a great majority of our self-assessment status, comes from a calculation of how we are doing in the path we have already set, in the mould which has been cast in part by our surroundings and its' agenda.

The important thing to notice here, is that although the end-product is to find in what direction the individual wishes to make efforts for themselves, without which there would be no fuel in the engine, a lot of this comes from an absorption of a collective judgmental system. We all have personal preferences and favourite things, which differ from each other, but in terms of our general menu of motivator goalposts, we rarely start from a blank sheet. The collective aspirations of a society are in general in the same ball-park. This is not written in stone, you may wish to live in tent on a diet of raw hedgerow as your ultimate satisfaction, but the probability of this is very low. We usually take on a collective general direction, as can be seen by comparing different societies from different countries and from different centuries.

In a society not as individualistic, the frameworks fix your role a bit more permanently. With this comes the emotional cost of having at least some of your aspirations being dictated to you. This happens in theory anyway, usually in a culture where this would not be a surprise. Pride and devotion to a communist state means you are not at liberty to decide upon everything you see as desirable, and also gives you a part of your self a sense of identity, which a true individualist would have no version of. In a very much less egoistic manner, part of your identity is from the outside of yourself, in a communal group ethos, which you are supposed to adhere to. If this were to happen in the 'west', the retraction of some of our ideological liberties would be very quickly felt in an electric knee-jerk, making a host of bleeps. Here, instead we are in a collective ethos that you're in a free-for-all to decide for yourself what matters or not. In contrast to their theoretical opposites, the individualist deems effort and expression needed to define their identity, which can be judged by others who are 'out for themselves' as well, whereas the communist individual is given a collective purpose which gives them some of their identity as a 'participant' in that collective action. Both of these scenarios are made by groups of people, thus the irony that individualists do come in herds. The big difference being that the effort in one is directed at self-attainment, and in the other the goal is collective action. This is mentioned here, not as a political analysis of the social-economic co-ordination engineered by different systems, purely a psychological observation of the footholds of identity in contrasting ideologies and their cultures.

Modern, western individualism, as a societal mindset, differs in comparison to other frames of mind in other places and times. The term can be used in different contexts, but the application in this westernized consumerist instance, can show relevance of the economic activity as a prime directive in our identity. This is quite a significant statement, if looked at from a more holistic perspective. How we label ourselves and expect others to identify us, is now more closely related to our purchasing power and choice of objects to possess, than it has been previously. This is a great simplification of the individual, being in the market place along with all the others, entirely driven by their own wishes. But, for example, a few hundred years ago, your place in the agricultural workforce, or work as a servant to a governor, would not just have obvious connections with your limits of access to material wealth, but would signify your role in society at almost all levels of human existence. Who's laws you were directed by and in what different places you would or would not be expected to be seen, your life expectancy and ability to travel in any comfort, were easy to estimate given your position in society. This was usually however connected to a hierarchy, of which you would be a part. Here your identity, not entirely, as you may have been a liar and very tall, was as part of a collective machinery which would have many intertwined features. Status had a lot to do with wealth, but had a lot of other factors, mostly to do with heritage. Whether society is fairer and has more equal opportunities now, is open to debate as hierarchies of advantage still exist, and as higher education becomes more widespread, it can be monitored to see how these qualifications alone may not alter the disparities in peoples' futures, related to which postcode they were born in.

The most positive aspect of individualism, is that in theory, this kind of historic divergence of possibilities is not supposed to be there. Ethnic background, choice of leisure activities, religion, are not connected to the ability of a person to prove how affective they can make themselves, in what choice of particular endeavor they have chosen for themselves. The paradigm of the responsibility of the well-being of the 'agent', being down to themselves, without circumstance being applicable, brings with it no tolerance for discrimination based on stereotypes of groups. The number of dominant factors, has been reduced to a simplification with materialistic attainment being the main anchor. This universal application of something so obvious can have a side-effect of providing a common ground of measure without there being exclusivity to its' use. General stereotypes of success or status being directly related to a hierarchical class system of birth, has in modern times diminished, all be it a lot more so psychologically than materially. The way we identify status is by the financial position of the individual, as a simple signifier of attainment quite accessible to the outsider to have a guesstimate at, just by using their material display and gate. This doesn't define 'class', but it does make a simple display of status. We all have more philosophical abilities to use than this crude and shallow judging mechanism, but it works in our society, so we do. It is also part of our common language of thought, without other factors such as considerateness or wisdom being needed very often. The label here through which we seek to identify someone's standing, is their attainment, being limited in its' scope by its' very nature. Sometimes, people can break the mould and use their own personality to interpret and display the great soup of variety around them. But this doesn't change what in general is culturally cohesive, not necessarily as a form of making judgmental decisions, but as an identifier that makes compartmentalisation a normal reflex in unconscious assessments.

As can be seen, we are trying to clarify the operating mechanisms in what can be described as individualism. It is with a broad brush we are trying to depict this, so it is excusable that much of the above does not allow for the fact that there is a huge amount of variance from person to person, still within the bounds of this being the way things are. Wants and desires have come to show more immediateness. Along with attention spans getting shorter, this is a cultural shift. One aspect of individualism is that this sense of identity has a persuasive effect on our mental framework, guiding our priorities over short and longer time-frames. The paradigm of 'making something of your life' being the hinge point of activity, like a blank sheet which it is up to you to fill in, will then define what you are. This puts a parameter around your existence, the end of that life being the end of that meaning. That is quite a bit away from the here and now, but nevertheless, has a large effect on what we take to be the things which matter. Again, this is not a conscious calculation of where to draw a line, but it is not so far fetched to see a connection between a paradigm which centres on the individual, and an unconscious personal ideology that doesn't focus on much other than your own life, in space and time. This however, is accompanied by a motivator which is 'get, have, do'. To obtain the material signifiers is a core driver in the majority of activities, which is exactly what does give preferences to the 'here and now' thinking. Self-centred is a less positive way of describing the individualist mindset. Attainment and achievement are good goals in life to have. The link this has to defining identity, has however, a diminishing effect on things which don't have such a direct causal link from the effort made to the getting of things - such as creativity, dignity, sharing and enjoyment. Sometimes things come by accident, when pondering something, the answer to something else can come to light. Gaining skills at one thing done purely for the sake of it, can lead to a knowledge that can be used elsewhere. These are not recommendations, just showing that the simplification of desire into end-goals only, being got at by pushing that thing which will obtain it, is a function which works, but if amplified by a framework of interaction and communication which rarely diverts from this logic, hinders diverse and progressive, personal development. If this is accepted as a normal mindset by a collective unconscious code of conduct by society, this is limiting culturally. Having the freedom to express ourselves individually is great, but the extent to which, mostly without knowing it, this leads us towards the paradigm that all of our concerns should only be focused inwardly as well, is a hindrance on the broad spectrum humans should be proud to have access to.

In defining your own character in terms of the attainment comparisons you can make with the cohabitants of your local environment, the important part that little effort is made towards enabling, is that communal surrounding atmosphere. It is very hard to get a sense of belonging and well-being, if your own and everyone else's attention is focused on a personal field of vision and accomplishment. We can all be cogs in a bigger machine, but if no-one does more than think that, the machine is not going to have a very beautiful design. Evolving from lots of cogs which don't bother to collaborate very well in anything beyond tolerance is restrictive. This isn't necessarily about money, or jobs, or politics, just what as individuals we consider to be the constructive substance we think an individual is made out of. To believe that the only social cohesion, is in a mutual agreement to pretend to care about each other in order to maximize our access to personal gains as an individualist, is a great equation, but forgets to ask what a real sense of belonging is made out of psychologically. Recognizing this, is not to declare a devotion to an entirely communal existence, just an understanding that there is a sliding scale that goes in both directions. The reason in the West we have gone so far down the route of withdrawing from collective citizenship, is that we found our identities not being given expressive or materialistic rewards in a previously demarcated mix of hierarchies. But, in as much as not being given your deserving reward, as an individual in a collective harvest, can be demoralizing, so can having a great payment in a world where everyone else's doors are closed.

Attractive delusion

Attractive delusion

Naaaa, y'know wot…..

USUAL RESPONSES

In the previous chapters, we saw that there is an increasing amount of noticeable side-effects of unwanted pollution. A simple reaction to being questioned about this, is to ask what the appropriate response to this could be. Why not investigate what are the best methods of reducing this pollution. This, however, is one of the least popular reactions given by any individual.

When in conversation, the concept of anthropocentrically caused climate change is met by a range of responses, which are usually more of a personal self-defense, against what is perceived as being an accusation of a moral violation. After seeing what is out there in the field of responses, we might be able to see what judgments, justifications or subconscious triggers are behind these usual replies, to clarify what is a wide spectrum of formats.

Volcanoes can come at any time, so thinking we can do anything is daft as that would be nothing in comparison.

It doesn't matter, as there will be an ice age soon anyway.

Once they sort out water-powered cars (or other things) that will make things OK.

It's not fair to ask people to give up what they have worked hard for and enjoy doing, pollution is inevitable.

I already recycle quite a lot.

I can't give a lot of time to worrying about that, I'm already…..

Its' all part of a natural cycle, humans aren't creating a problem, over millions of years it has always done that.

Putting the brakes on a productive economy is a bad idea, we need to keep the economy going.

People who worry about the planet make that stuff up to give themselves something to rant about.

God (or other non-human powers) will make things how they're supposed to be, if everything gets hot, that's what he wants.

What is the point in us trying to change things when China is making a new coalmine every five minutes.

We don't know if it's going to happen or not yet, those scientists just make half of it up to getting paid to do more research.

It doesn't exist as a problem, the government like having it as a way of excusing more taxes on loads of things.

Well it might be true, but I'll be gone by then, I suppose my grandchildren should think about it.

Dinosaurs went extinct, these things happen.

What we can see, as a generalisation, is that there is a lot of what is commonly called scepticism. The water-powered cars example though, shows a belief in there being a technical solution, which could in some ways be hopeful. The vast majority though are not in this ballpark, they tend to be hinting at the hopelessness of effort, or a dismissal of the problem as not worth considering. It is possible to categorize this into different areas of belief format. A simple compartment, with obvious consequence, is the belief that the situation of the climate changing causing negative side effects, doesn't exist. Problem solved, because there isn't one. Almost the opposite of this, are diversionary moves. These beliefs lead to a judgment that proposes that there is an issue, but once a responsive element comes into play, this shows that the subject should come off the table of personal concern.

It is interestingly apparent though, that what is hardly ever encountered, is what would be a calm rational response to a simple question about the future of the world and pollution. This could be something along the lines of - Is there a situation and if so where and when are the repercussions? - Are we at a reasonable level of understanding the possible outcomes and solutions? - What information would help us come to a good level of confidence that we have a good grasp of what we are dealing with? Unfortunately, this absence of clarity is true on all sides of a crazy fence. Environmentalists, despite being emotionally connected to taking measures to remedy the onset of harm, rarely describe what the actual consequences are they are trying to help us avoid. Understandably, they usually become annoyed at how most people deny its' existence and avoid even thinking about possible solutions. The questions and answers on the subject, seem to be either dismissed entirely, swept under a sideways rug, or argued about in an emotional tangle, brought about by the lack of clarity surrounding the whole issue. This should highlight that what we are investigating here, is a subject, which stirs up peoples emotional, psychological platforms for response, which is very different to when someone is calculating the answer to something simplistic or dry.

We can categorise most of the responses encountered, into four different type-casts. 'Flat-earthers' deny the existence of climate change, using what is quite an extreme way of dealing with something, by removing it completely from the judgement arena. This would not be recommended on other issues such as an overdraft or a house fire, but is a very popular mind-set on this subject. 'Responsibility-removers' take many number of different side-steps, taking the disruptive element of pollution out of the way, without denying its' existence. 'Depressive observers' have a good grasp of reality, with a special gift for the cold bit of cold-rationality, which unfortunately comes at the price of an emotionally expensive awareness of the potential doom, accompanied by a correlating mood. A fourth but rarely encountered option are the 'morally defunct', whom, out-loud, wear their heartlessness on their sleeve by declaring others' welfare as uninteresting, thus narrowing the margin of concern about pollution to their own well-being. The differences between these types of thought processes are interesting for us to compare and study, as it clarifies the otherwise murky waters. But, these definitions do not entirely encapsulate people from one to another, as quite often a lot of people flit from one kind of reaction to another, to suit their own purposes, or to fit the situation. It also doesn't entirely explain why our culture or society has helped to mould people into such formats, and has done so without there being an arousal of a conspicuous alarm bell. The following categories are therefore a generalisation, but what is noticeable, is that they very much cover the majority of reactions to the subject, all of them being very different from an inquisitiveness or putting energy towards finding the truth. Potential solutions, would in normal circumstances, if asked objectively, be an anticipated response. The reason the spectrum of beliefs is so sensitive to emotional inputs, is that even without saying anything related to this in the questioning of this subject, the response is felt by the participant to be a moral issue. Here is where the axis of belief starts to wobble.

Scientific denial, or the belief that the problems caused by pollution, are fictitiously created by scientists, is a surprisingly large proportion of beliefs. The popularity of denial, doesn't make it true. The interesting point here, is whether this is accidental or deliberate. This belief system is only now starting to become recognized as delusional. For twenty years it has kept rearing its head into the popular forum of the 'is it - isn't it' debate. At one time, a media organization made a comment that there may be the need to notify the audience as to the status of the credibility of the information in its' reliability of source. It was needed in order to avoid popularizing unrealistic doubt when broadcasting an ideology in this area. Some public voices are clearly seen as interesting, controversial, but lacking any balance in terms of likeliness to represent a well informed judgment. The largeness of this belief format, gives us inspiration to look at the proportion of which may be innocently misguided by pseudo information delivery. The opposite of this is the use of actual mental effort to maintain a belief despite contrary evidence, sometimes subconsciously guided to take this action. 'Flat Earthers' have a cognition system we can recognise as biased by motivation and emotion, and this steers reality off course, usually for their own short-term benefits.

There is a slight difference here between those that have initiated the motive to delude themselves, and those that accidentally come to acquire a belief, but refuse to let it change, despite contrary evidence. For reasons of alignment of ideas, in both of these scenarios, there is a subconscious occurrence of self-regulation. This may be by ignoring or diverting contrary evidence, which is very much under the umbrella of cognitive dissonance. Flat-earthers have the opinion that the issue is non-existent ethically, as do, by different means, 'the miss-informed', who are made unaware of the situation. A large part of this, in the modern world, being due to the way the issue has been dealt with by the media. An interesting observation about this standpoint, is that when someone tells me about their deciding-point of knowledge on climate change, is that 'that kind of things has always happened', which therefore means there is no need for concern as nature is bouncing along with or without humans as it always has, can after a short clarifying commentary on the state of play, be followed by a 'it's too late to do anything about it'. The noteworthy part of this, is the irony of the one hundred and eighty degree turn. From the thing not being real at one moment, it then becomes very real and an all too powerful dawn of doom the next. This shows where the **effectiveness** of not very good or accurate information, comes from. There is something needed by the conclusion, which is anchored on 'action or concern are unwarranted', therefore demanding the necessary bits be filled in forthwith. Whether this means swinging to the left or right doesn't matter so long as it ends up in the right place. This does differ however, from the entrenched fervency with which some flat-earthers dig their heels in. Guided very much by their internal motivations, not the information presented to them, the conclusion of the earth being flat, and not getting warmer due to human activity, will not shift. Here the conclusion, and the preferred means of getting to it, are fixed. These people will in no way tolerate the unwanted variable complicating their agenda, and will go to great effort to find the supporting data and justifications, which is in this case on a specific evidence area, not just a designated moral outcome.

An alternative mindset, with an energetic amount of knee-jerking, rapid response, are the morally defunct, some of which could be described as 'ethical nihilists'. These people are in the category of 'aint no problem', but not because they believe there will not be any negative side-effects from pollution, but because their own welfare is not going to be seriously affected, and that is all that matters to them. This is a large categorical change in type of judgment from straight flat-earthing. Making a moral decision that something does not matter, makes the issue go into non-existence for the self, independently of the application of any one else's ability to care. Flat-earthers remove the subject from requiring moral thought by taking it out of being part of any reality, as it is then not real for anyone. Unlike this, the morally defunct leave it in reality, but decide that they do not wish to apply morality. This envelope of people is a bit larger than only those subject to an unusually inconsiderate frame of thinking, if it is to include all those that consider the subject as morally expedient. We must be careful here, to keep the morally defunct separate from those that use different methods to weigh up the consequences in different ways. In this situation, there is no moral question, not because other people in this or other places, now or in the future, are not going to suffer, but because there is no need to take this into consideration. This would include the 'I'll be dead by then', so its' not my problem, where the calculation of any cost or benefit has been jettisoned by drawing a line at ones' own existence. How the variables of space and time play significant roles in our moral judgments, is very important on the particular issue of how much concern we show for people in the future in different parts of the world, who are in some ways effected by our activities now.

An obvious form of cognitive self-service when confronted by this unwanted questioning, is to keep one's head in the sand. Pure ignorance is not admirable, but not dysfunctional, as this is not a decision making process or judgment. Deliberate blinkers are justifiable in some situations, but not usually. The simplicity of head in the sand, does however have an honesty of limiting information, compared to the mind bending of flat-earthers, that don't hide from the truth, but bend it into a suitable shape. What we could label as not being admirable though, is that the individual in this case, has the ability to see what is implied from rational deliberation, but would prefer to avoid this conclusion by deliberately blocking the relevant information. It is not unacceptable to want to keep a distance from painful conclusions, but that cannot make it a desirable attribute of a person. There are situations which justify not inviting more negativity, but that is because the person is already suffering in some way. This differs however, from not limiting the unintentional negative side-effects of your own actions, by remaining in a state of deliberate ignorance. This is particularly unlikely to be worn as a decision made in public, if it becomes clear that the suffering accidentally caused is going to be landing on other people. An honest more ethical appraisal of the situation, could be to remove some of the burdensome amount of information. The persons' deliberation on things, can be to approve of these matters being dealt with in an accompanying jurisdiction without the need for your own personal input. This would be a combination of self-aware, misinformed ignorance with a trust in authority, making keeping one's head in the sand a more satisfactory stance. As is apparent though, this appeal of what could become legislation or guidelines, is counteractive to the attraction of a 'free as possible' free market of self expression.

There is a lot of people who have a situation of judgment, that does not introduce a concept of dysfunctional morality application, or expose deviant information processing. These people may be consumers of goods and services that have some negative side effects, which is unintentional. When informed of these consequences, they nevertheless remain in the same pattern of behaviour, and do not allow this additional factor into their decision-making procedure. 'Powerless' is a relatively negative concept, but quite appropriate in the area of environmental concern, if the individual is in a tight spot, where they really don't have the opportunity to consider these variables as accessible. Poverty would be a good example. It might be true that someone in this situation could, if well planned, change their diet to bioregional, organic, affordable alternatives to their usual choices. But given the level of stress, suffered in the maintenance of any type of well-being, it is not appropriate to judge their decision-making equipment at all. In this situation the person can be considered as innocent, even if there are unnecessary negative side effects resulting from their actions. Most of us are to some extent in this area of judgment, where we have not dug to the most minute of details, to pollution-wise purify our actions. In this way there is a grey area of awareness as well as the direction of choices. A familiar niche is the 'too busy' syndrome. This area however, can be a deliberate 'head in the sand' approach. Being wealthy, and busy arranging expensive consumerist behaviors, does not justify the concept of having a reasonable explanation to ignore any morality that is counterproductive to one's own indulgencies. A person in this zone would probably respond in an angry manner, if they were asked if they considered themselves to be 'powerless' to respond to ethical factors, as the driving motivational force behind the sweeping aside of environmental concerns is a sense of self-importance, verified by their wealth. This can be held as a personality trait where the mess they create is up to other people to clean up, down to their superiority of supposed status. This can be contrasted with the powerless through poverty, which does carry with it very real justifications for not giving any time or effort to being concerned over unwanted side effects.

Some people just go back to their position of 'problem denial' after a bit of time. This would be a sign of 'slow-mind bending'. Here contrary evidence has been considered, and then later on avoided or ignored, using a bit of a back-burner process. Sometimes, there would be a self-defence mechanism, where a new proposition is presented as showing that the evidence going in the non-preferred direction has inadequacy of proof. This is where 'bias' becomes an active response, needing mental effort to compose supporting data and counter-evidence. Rather than change from a 'there is no problem' to a 'there is a problem' person, the individual comes up with a series of defences showing that their mind is not open in the long-term, to possibilities that conflict with their preference of not having to worry about something. How to judge whether this is actually what can be thought about this stage of someone's thinking, would need reasonable evidence that the conclusion is not getting there from an objectively balanced deliberation. The interesting thing not being this, but what is it that motivates them to stick to their existent conclusion. What is worth noting at this stage, is that we are looking at peoples usual responses, and taking apart what these reactions are made of. This doesn't entirely criticize each individual for taking these particular stances, as we are in general exploring a larger field of enquiry - as to where do the triggers for these responses come from, and at the more social, psychological level, looking from a cultural perspective as to what direction things are supposed to be heading in, and how do they inspire these mind-sets.

There are though, some people who are able to cope with a realm of reality, where there are some unfortunate side effects to some of their behavior, which is allowed into their space of contemplation. As can be expected, this remains undesirable. Two techniques of avoiding the attachment of responsibility to choices are displacement and dislocation. Both of these are **responsibility removers.** It is not unexpected, that people who are capable of inhabiting a zone separate from flat-earthers, sub-consciously desire a technique of keeping themselves from complicating their decision making with external influences that usually restrict their choices in a less enjoyable direction. This is not to say that environmentally considerate lifestyles are necessarily less enjoyable, it is just that the most common patterns of judgment and behavior are not complicated by this factor, which makes diversions from this extra complication quite desirable.

Displacement is an easy and simple technique. It is not often scientifically accurate, but is a response formation that can discourage external influences, usually criticism from an outsider. A good example would be dissolving criticism that one's car is unnecessarily mountain proof, with the admission that one is concerned with global consequences of carbon emissions, but adhering to the principle that by recycling some of the packaging of consumer goods, one is already making a contribution to reducing climate change, therefore displacing oneself from the decision area of needing to worry about the choice of motor-vehicle. This is scientifically counterproductive. When presented with simple carbon numbers, the evidence is quite simple. But the interesting thing is the use of a technique to offset one's own guilt, without any desire to understand how to accurately apply it. This shows the motivation to deflect criticism, for reasons which are other than desiring accurate understanding of the subject. 'I recycle quite a lot though', full stop. Off-setting is a real principle, which in theory could work. More often than not though, the idea is that a box can be ticked which will displace any further need for thought. What is interesting, is that removing responsibility is less popular than the simple flat-earth response, but can be a follow-up to flat-earthing if it seems less credible. From very different moral perspectives, one denying the existence of any moral ground, and the other giving it consideration, they both end up in the conclusion of not being disrupted from their usual perspective in decision making. As I think will become clearer, this is the effect of the over-riding principle of consumerism, this being incompatible with the idea of choices being relevant to decisions beyond personal desire being present in our activity in the market place.

Different to this technique, but sometimes held in unison, is dislocation. When considering the problems probably arising from carbon emissions, the scale of the problem can be used to dislocate oneself from the responsibility zone. This is often the power of numbers. It is quite acceptable to not blame oneself for the less favourable government being elected, as you only have one vote. This does not however make one thousand wrongs a right. It is true that one vote doesn't make a lot of difference, but that doesn't make it justifiable to vote for the Nazis. However, it is not unexpected, that when presented with large-scale problems, as an individual, one feels quite constrained as to how much influence your own decisions can make. In this way, it is a useful tool to conceptualize a problem as beyond your control, and in that way you can join the herd without problem solving any moral dilemma. 'There is a problem, but there's nothing I can do about it', is obviously very close to the truth, as we can tell from the numbers game. It is clear though that the problem will persist, if there is faith in the concept that what everyone should do, is nothing but be spectators.

One example of this frame of thinking in the West, is to cite the large quantities of pollution caused by other countries. Although it may be true that China is manufacturing a large number of coal-fired power stations, the goal of the mindset is to remain deliberately powerless. When a huge amount of demerit is being made by lots of people a long way away, there is very little influence you can have. One small reference point worth making, is that for each person in China, each person in America produces five times that amount. That aside though, the mindset of an individual taking this tactic, is to make oneself appreciated, and respected for their open-mindedness and their ability to consider the evidence that there is this problem, but then to avoid making any personal changes which they might not desire, by dislocating oneself from the zone of ethical judgment. This decision will continue to be reinforced, in a layer of their belief system behind many of its' outcomes. However this is not by a conscious campaign motto to be dismissive, but an unconscious motivation to keep the operating system of thought running smoothly on the simplistic pattern already established. Having the objective of removing responsibility is not going to have any good effect on any attempt to clarify the state of the real world, but takes a lot of weight off the shoulders of many people who just want to get on without having to complicate their hopes to get further along their own happiness ladder.

These two tactics differ in their way of removing responsibility. Displacement makes the decision that they have already made a positive decision, which is significant enough to make any further action in this area unwarranted. Dislocation does the opposite, which is to consider harmful consequences to be taking place, but the cause of this harm being elsewhere, in which their own actions, which could considered bad, are not implicated.

The variables of space and time are simple, and yet critical to any conclusion that may arise when looking at the far-reaching subject of climate change. There is here reassuring evidence that most peoples' ethical rationality is in tact. Principles, and the following ethical judgments are at the disposal of most people. This involves how they may undertake the application of these, taking into consideration how far-off they are relevant. Contradictorily, and unexpectantly, we can see that this is highly likely in flat-earthers. They are aware of the train of thought that will follow from considering the consequences of pollution on the welfare of people all around the world in the future. The best tactic for this person with reasonable ethical equipment, who wishes to move away from this conclusion, usually unconsciously, as it is contrary to their desires to remain untroubled by this, is to cut this train off at its starting point of being part of reality.

This ethical tampering, even though our outlook may not have prioritized the development of long-range morality, continues into the zone of responsibility removers. Here, these people do not trim their level or range of ethical application, they simply move themselves out of the area of application by using dislocation or displacement. These people don't have dodgy ethical principles, what happens is they come to the conclusion that they have no control over the results and may therefore dislodge themselves from anything resembling responsibility.

Some displacers conclude they have already dealt with it. All of these are dispositions, are not in their make-up an in-depth analysis of a global conundrum, just more of a quick 'what do you think about...' reaction. This is not to underestimate that as being a *core driver*, they are very popular, and make the majority of the answers. This does not show that most people are inconsiderate, or don't have a moral mindset. It shows that they have reflex responses, which are effective at removing these long-range ethical dilemmas from troubling them. This is very natural, as we were not built to take into our judgment equipment the non-near-to-hand difficulties, unless we feel the need to give it our undivided attention.

Space and time are critical drivers, but not always at the rational level. Our ethical equipment is not corrupted, but usually tallied-up to work out we are not creating or suffering from any immediate danger, and then put to one side. Anthropology is an explanation that can be used. By uncovering the history of evolution of the brains that make judgments, it can be seen that we haven't evolved to prioritize long-range concern. By observing this, the forecast of downward movement of human welfare, is explainable objectively, and may be regrettable, but can be considered as expected. This allows one to choose to continue with the masses in the same direction, but only if your willing to accept an explanation as a justification for a downward spiral brought about by each other. Usually though we have a faith in something a bit more than a trudge down the inevitable. Respect for the dinosaurs doesn't mean you want to be one.

To accept unnecessary suffering of people in other places and other times, caused by our lack of ability to control our own actions, is at some level justifiable, but rarely vocalized, or even consciously understood. This is when we feel outweighed by others who wish to remain accidentally the cause of the same consequences as we do. Far easier than making an open admission, is to dislocate your own actions with an externalizing blame somewhere else, or by displacing your anxiety through some other action.

Three phrases which show where the driving force of the belief formation in this direction comes from, are 'business as usual', 'conservatism' and 'status-quo'. Making a change, is hard when looked at from the perspective of it being a normal social construct, leaving only minorities to move in a different direction. This is accepted a lot more, if the changes are small and easy to make. The principles of recycling household waste are no less complex than other externalities. This includes embodied energy and retrogressive material processes. But the idea of how you treat the no longer required packaging of other things, doesn't usually have a feeling of personal sacrifice. Energy supply, and transport systems, do however bring about a wrangle about what to do, as we have spent a lot of time growing accustomed to the existing way of things, and those things are out there now, which do what we want them to do. These social norms, put force to the concepts of displacement and dislocation. Again, not by twisting my ethical principles, the simple manoeuvre of pushing the issues I am not comfortable with to one side, using something else, helps me keep hold of my personal desires without the tinge of guilt.

The opposite to 'hot' psychological emotive responses, is cold rationality. One type of belief formation process, which typically has a lot of cold reflection, is what could be described as 'depressive observers'. Having either had in their past, a period of melancholy, or remaining in a 'downbeat' condition, these people may have a psychological framework enabling depressive realism. Some psychological studies have concluded that the ability of people to rationally process the information of a situation, can be enhanced to above average ability by those with this disposition. This is an example of accurate cold cognition, attention not being swayed in the usual ways with emotional influence. This is more commonly true when presented with relatively negative information. The persons' previous experience of things including negativity, has equipped them to handle the presentation of 'depressing' information in a cold rational way, having had either already dealt with something similar, or a similar feeling, by simply accepting the information as real, rather than being internally encouraged to twist or neglect the possibility of the information being part of reality. This is a positive, starting point of avoiding delusion. But these individuals are 'depressive observers', because there can be a negative side effect of their belief formation. Having the ability to rationally deal with doom, does not necessarily equip the person with a usual level of motivation, or ability to interact, in order to bring about a positive change in this area. Having a good ability to process the available information about the situation, is not just available to these people though. What we could stereotype as academics or scientists are also usually good at taking the evidence at face value, who are able to come to a reasonable understanding of the severity of the problems faced, and keep capable of communicating ones' ideas in a way that is not seen to be an incompassitating dark cloud. The truth can hurt, so how to handle it is an important factor in addition to coming to see it for what it is. For this reason, having a reasonable analysis of the most likely events in the future, and an ability to openly express ones' awareness of the negative outcome of a continuation of the existing path of progress, is a lot less popular than the many other paradigms which make change less likely.

People normally follow a flexible arrangement of sometimes getting a bit emotional, and sometimes not. The truth can get bent a bit, as inner guidance leads one's motivation to give preference to some conclusions. Attention may stay focused on information that would confirm the preferred hypothesis. Emotions may sometimes over-ride rational decision-making, leaving a more spontaneous reaction having to deal with the situation. These things that happen, may not have consistency, sound ethical application or a sound reflection of reality, but nevertheless this is still what we could consider 'normal'. We might consider this 'normality' a reckless state of being human, which could be prone to confusion. This is true, as it is of many imperfections. Being a 'hot and colder', means changes are probable, brought about by flexibility. People are often more complicated that our simple compartmentalized different formats. This attribute of changeability, can however be an accompaniment, to being an entrenched flat-earther, or a committed responsibility remover, or a deliberate head-in-sander, which provides a certain amount of consistency in the method of response, with adaptations and variability like all of us.

The desirability of variance within a normal flexibility can be seen. If climate change is an argument, there are not going to be any happy winners. The conclusions can be either that something unfortunate exists or that it doesn't, the latter being miss-guided. Either way though, I can't see it being likely that winning the argument either way, would make anyone jump up and down with joy. This makes it 'normal' to bat this thing about. It is very accessible to keep this inquisitive flexibility operating. But the desirability of any conclusion relating to doom, is low. Here we can see how most people respond to the issue, would usually be seen in a proportion to the general state of play in the current public arena. In a sense this shows impartiality, responding to surrounding information, which unfortunately has more to do with headlines than reality. There can be a positive side to environmentalism, the beauty of life causing the motivation to preserve it, the joy of providing well-being for others into a long-term sustainable future, but this is not what usually presents itself in discussion. The societal-radar normally keeps this subject off target. The difference between positive and negative, *in itself* and not attached to whatever subject it is imbedded in, is important. If the 'climate' is seen as an incoming attack on the 'so far successful' running of our current machine, and the means of dispelling this interruption are seen in a positive light with a sigh of relief that we can keep chugging on, this negative shadow helps to make the interrupter undesirable. What this adaptation of thought is bringing though, is relief from the pressure of 'making good' the damaging system. This is due in part to the concept of environmentally friendly measures, being unable to avoid having an aspect of 'ought to' or 'should' suggested in their nature. We can fix things, at some cost or at some effort, but the idea that this is an obligatory measure, in addition to our existent struggle for happiness, brings reluctance.

Morality is needed to work out what to do. Ethics is a wide subject, and if brought up in discussion when addressing a subject, leads to very interesting debates. This could be cultural relativism versus human rights. But what we have found in the wide spectrum of belief formats looked at here, is that this kind of debate, doesn't seem to come up. The psychological coping mechanisms don't open up the debate over what matters, to who, or when. It is more likely that the subject is put in a box and shoved to one side, or recognized as real and depressing, which makes most people want to leave it in the box. We have seen where some of the reasons for this, many of them in the unconscious judgments that we all make, come from. We have managed to make this a bit clearer here, in a few pages. Our modern society has plenty of time to comment upon itself in the media all day, which happens to be walking towards unnecessary suffering on a global scale, so far without showing much of a hindrance to this reality. What is it that is causing an inability to bring out an honest appraisal and discuss adaptation? Globally, agreements have been made. This shows reality is starting to get heard. But these agreements are very hard for politicians to take home with any real obligation for action, when the general background noise there is from a very different orchestra. So where has morality gone, and why?

Attractive delusion

Attractive delusion

A defiant herd of pointy-nosed plastic stand-offs

POWER OF THE HERD

As consumers, we all have our freedoms to choose what it is we desire, and thereby encourage its' occurrence, either in knowledge of the side-effects of its' creation or not. Most of what we buy, however, are already in a chain of events deemed as desired by the collective action of lots of people of which we are a tiny part. In a way, this could be taken as the social responsibility being made on mass, leaving our personal psychological decision making at some distance removed. However, the decision of the merit of the goods or services provided, is exactly what a personal choice does, just the same as a vote. But, the scale of the decision is at a social level and forms the cultural platform, from which, mostly unconsciously, our decisions are made. This is the mindset of our society and has the power of a very strong herd.

The use of an existing framework, does provide a huge convenience, in not having to trouble oneself about anything by adding complications to choosing what one wishes to have or do. This hugely efficient part of reality is quite often investigated to see what does become activated by these decisions, to reveal unwanted events brought about by the chain of events in the provision of these things. For example, cheap sweatshop products, illegal drug production. So it is not unheard of to find unwanted side-effects from buying things. In many ways, the things we desire, have been given a status by their having a symbolism of desirability, given to it by a collective action stood hard in place without our input, delivered in part by its' availability. Some decisions we make, have already be made for us. Our belief in the free-market, makes it feel as if it comes from the heart through our decision making, but in part we are just content to be in the pack that is already heading in that direction. The important thing to notice, is that what doesn't happen, is that when we are making individual personal psychological moves, these do not then feel as judged at the social level to see if this brings about responsibility for good or ill effects. The psychological headspace, is relieved of this in the social sphere, as a collective paradigm. The availability of the good or service on the market, means it has been collectively deemed as being suitable for us to use or consume if we so desire. Unfortunately, the results of our current programme of our wants and desires, fed by our consumer based free-market, is creating a quantity of pollution which has damaging effects on the planet and the welfare of a lot of people on it. There is harm from the rapid changes in weather patterns and the temperature of the climate.

There is harm, which reduced pollution would reduce, which is usually not taken into consideration when we make the simple choices of what things we want or desire. Things are deemed as acceptable because they are available. The harder part is then seeing if you have enough money to have these things we want, after stylistically blending them in with your self-identity and motivations. Not to leave unnoticed also though, is that climate change is not the only issue which may trouble people, leading to personal boycotts or moral dilemmas over different things, for varied, sometimes political or religious reasons. This also shows how our observations on the usual psychological patterns of consumerism, does not universally define everyone, is more of a social generalisation within which people vary. The climate is however, something we are all under and all affecting, with which we have, given our history of response, a conspicuous inability to accept as either real or manageable. So here we are looking at only one issue, but the psychological pattern of moral concerns not being automatically enlivened by consumer based decisions, is equally applicable elsewhere.

Is this process of wanting things, having them, and unwarily causing damage, hard to change? Not really. It is a complication, which happens to be beyond cost or desirability. Basically, it is a factor, which could be added in, but at this time in history, usually isn't. Sometimes things do cost more to produce in environmentally friendly ways, but sometimes they cost less – it is purely a new variable, which could be factored in, because if it isn't, we will continue to bring about unnecessary harm. If this is seen as an unwanted complication, things could be justified by different means. Special occasions, or tricky situations, can be seen on balance with a bit of leeway. The simple batting off, using 'don't worry about that', which dispenses with this inconvenient variable, is a more common reflex response, which works unconsciously. Again however, this is not normally an individuals' singular psychological process, it is more of a collective, social understanding. This pollution factor is seen as not required and is dispensable, which is easy to see the motivation for, as there is little inspiration to add blame or responsibility into this pleasure of desire and attainment. We are looking at this occurrence in two ways at the same time. By analysing the situation and the consequential results of this culturally popular paradigm, we are dissecting reality and comparing it to a rational response. An equally interesting point though, is to look at why this prevails as part of normality, and where this thinking pattern comes from.

What we have as a normal subconscious framework for decision making, is the idea of the 'liberty of the free market' bringing shared prosperity by our individually following self-interest. We have been informed that the greater good will happen, by using the trading of goods and services and getting money to take part in this. In many ways this is true and is successful. While looking at the hitches, it is worth remembering about the great benefits that have come from this phenomenon, which does generate its' embedded, likely survival. But, it is not a blanket designed to cover everything. There are some things this system is not suitable for, and consequently, the constant use of this mind-set has degraded our ability to apply collective responsibility to things which don't coincide with our short-term self-interest. This is why the idea of working together to reduce pollution, without lowering our standard of living, is met with incredulity. When 'greed is good' is a close analogy to what is in the back of everyone's mind, less of anything, including things that are not desirable, doesn't seem relevant or motivational. These are bitter statements to make, as they are about our current state of mind. But if this is not the case, what we have here is a simple phenomenon to inspect and discuss. This is also not a critique of our ability to be different from this, or to portion blame for going this way, more an analysis of what the current state of play is, albeit with its' shortfalls.

The use of the free-market, making exchange of goods and services flow smoothly and bringing its' own efficiency, or 'the invisible hand' as named by Adam Smiths in the 'Wealth of Nations', comes with what he himself saw to be the limits to the compatibility of when this should be allowed to be the principle guidance system. From this we can conclude that from the outset, the principles of free-trade were not seen as having the ability to always operate without glitches, or at worst are unsuitable. Modern living and the emerging problems of climate and pollution, brings about two different symptoms of there being defects allowed to prevail. The noticeable effect of the difficulties is that there is a thing which needs to be fixed. Whether this is through market forces or government regulation, or even consumer choices, there is something going wrong and there is a need for change. Unless we are expected to embrace the short-term individualist ideology to the level of the self without any regard for anyone else, particularly people younger than ourselves, or in a different, most-at-risk country, this should be seen as a system failure. The other symptom, is not physical, but psychological. How is it that we are unaware of how our cultural thinking patterns and activities have made this happen, and cause reflex responses which don't allow this to be recognised or rectified, for the purpose of the 'greater good' we were supposed to be conducted by?

The invisible side-effect of consumerist libertarianism, is that the invisible hand has been trusted to such an extent, that our ability to show consideration has gone to sleep. The free movement of personal desires through the efficient market forces, provides a justification for consumerism. This unfortunately can also serve to repress our natural ability to care about our surroundings enough to keep our desires in check, even if not to directly hinder them. This disposition, is more often than not, defended by an emotional trigger, which even if this shortfall is only suggested, has a response of a rebuttal. To say that our levels of empathy or care are hindered by the automation of our transaction processes, is difficult to accept. When this comment on our usual paradigm is detected, we have an automatic inhibition to allow any of this destabilizing to occur. The arena of this activity does not like disruption. This is the principle nature of the response, not a complicated cost-benefit analysis of the after-effects of a recalibration of decision making procedures; and why not, freedom from bother is something we are all drawn to.

One example of the reasoning that it can provoke though, is more emotional thought on the concept of unwanted authoritarian interference. The result this leads to, is that we are powerless as individuals to guide the whole free-market, and also empowered to not care about complications if we wish things to be so. The assumption, is usually that we cannot stop the march of the crowds we are part of, meaning the only thing which could redirect this large swathe of activity would be government control, which is usually, in terms of the emotional field, not on the list of acceptable courses of action. The emotional trigger that has been pulled, is to take this criticism as a negative analysis of the direction of the herd, and that the accuser should back off from pointing their finger at this particular individual, who is not in control of this enormity. The direction society has chosen to take, is taken as not to be questioned, or if it is, this is not at the personal/individual level you can be held accountable for. This makes yourself, powerless to change things on the one hand, and free from criticism about choices one makes from within this on the other. A deviation from this is to take an unacceptable personal slant.

The thing that has been given away to the invisible hand, is control. The need to double check, investigate or show any interest in, any of the things behind the closed doors of the delivery of the products to your shopping bag, has disappeared from conscious thought, giving the individual freedom to make choices at a personal level with differing thoughts of how this interacts with other things outside of this zone, off the table. This has come from trust in the service delivered by the free market. As a collective policy, it is not questioned, and if it is, the 'we are all in it', does give us a sense of how psychologically this is kept at a level of belief that is not to be disturbed, particularly as its' existence is as a group ideology of society. A lot of this powerfulness comes from this freedom, from both constraint and having to think, that is brought by this disposition. However, this comes at a cost, because at least in our minds, no matter what political persuasion you are, this mass of individuals cannot be guided, encouraged, educated, informed or in any way influenced on this subject, without resenting this as unwarranted interruption from an unrepresentative power. The main involvement we all have is to be complicit in an unstoppable wave, and usually, quite happy to be so. This is self-interest, but how much of this is at the conscious, versus the unconscious level of judgment, is something which takes some thought to uncover. The way that a lot of reactions are so sudden, shows how it is not the factual deliberation over the subject matter, (the example being of production processes and pollution) it is the psychological discomfort of having the simple uncomplicated arena of consumerist choices being interrupted by a variable (that may contain more serious tones of ethical judgments, which if contravened, would be a detrimental to the persons' status of character), that causes the sudden repulsion, pushing this possible judgment out of the personal zone.

    Not the only, but one prevalent reaction to the pollution factor interference, is the assumption that the proposed counteractive action to this difficulty, would be to install diligent government regulations, which will restrict harm-causing processes, along with which the consumers personal liberties would also be limited. This is not wholly incorrect as a feasible prescriptive answer, but it is also not necessary. There are many alternative routes of change, once the dilemma has been accepted as real. It does show however, that when we question the outcomes of the consumerist market, the reaction is not to question the consumer and the direction of their freely made choices. As individualists (in a consumer based society), we feel we are expressing ourselves and our identity by the consumerist choices we make, which distinguish us from others in the surrounding community-level thinking. Choices are personal, in both whom they are from and where the zone of consideration is focused on. When making these personal statements through having and buying things, the mind does not wander into a field of operation beyond the self. This is helpful and efficient, as in a lot of things, this is all that is relevant. This limit to what level of thinking is used, is though, unconsciously, welcomed. It does not become apparent that a tactic is chosen which is limiting mental activity, as it is not presented as a choice whether to do so or not. The same is true for many historical changes in perception and attitude. A choice is not consciously made, it is more a cultural norm that swings in that direction without any noticeable Copernican moment. If things are right or wrong, harmful or even pointless, these questions are not in the zone of consumerism. That is considered for another time and a different kind of state of mind. An attractive proposition presented by this cultural perspective, is that all the complications of morality are in a different field. If all consumer activity, had a cost-benefit analysis accompanying it, that would be a very annoying, long complicated process. Rejection of this is appealing. But, with the current mind-set, this has actually made most of care and consideration get turned off, in order to get on with the pace of a 'get this do that' life, which is a consequence of the unimpeded desire based, consumerist strategy.

The above referrals to consumer choice, is mostly showing what is unconsciously implied by normal shopping. In a way, the unknown and undesirable consequences are commissioned by our purchasing power. We take part in a normal activity of choosing to have some of things we want. Ethical shopping is possible, which could be a great avenue for progress. The observation here though is that this would be far from normal. In a society collectively committed to consumerism, the culture has more positive responses to individualism than to morality. The bias is in the field of operation. Consumption choices in their applicability to identity taking most of the spotlight, makes the involvement of ethical choices a bit like trying to do the same thing whilst standing on one leg, as these forms of thinking are very different styles of judgment.

Other examples of influential parts of our lifestyle, which are commercial, are not so obviously retail, and have more noticeable cause and effect connections with the environmental world. Heating our homes and transport both have pollution as direct side-effects, which is much more apparent than in other consumer activities. These aspects of our lives are however not psychologically segregated from consideration in the same way as shopping. The side-effects of these things are conspicuous, in the emissions generated by them. But more interestingly is a correlation between the amount of fuel running through them and the cost of putting this fuel into these things to have the desired outcome they are there for. Here we have examples of what should stir in the mind an inquisitive approach to reducing the input and the cost to deliver the same outcome. Consensus of the herd should be at its' most sensitive point to adaptation here. These parts of our lives are considerably different psychologically in terms of a natural feeling of the responsibility of consequences, than in simply buying something from a shop. But like many of the choices we make, these areas don't come with the freedoms that would imply we would take responsibility for their selection. The heating of your home, and the transport you choose to use, have direct consequences, but the choices which are apparent to the consumer as being available, may feel somewhat limited. The way in which in normal consumer based activity is kept simple and focused on personal desires and preferences, is not there in the choice of a heating system. The desire is not to burn gas at all, or use electricity, the end-goal being the other things such as warmth or having the device turn on and off to do what is required. The physical chain of events is more apparent than in goods and services produced at a distance, but the 'side-effects' are still just that, and not a direct choice. It is the limitations determined by normality that make the liberty of choice in which source of fuel or energy to use, seem far off from my personal choices. This is very much herd activity, as it is not up to me which raw materials go into what energy is available for me to use in the local area, and the consensus in what type of transport is most viable, for example, in there being roads and not tram-lines, and other ready made networks, which is guiding available choices. So we have a more instinctive awareness of the pollution that is made by our choices, that is very different from normal consumerism, but are train-tracked into limited avenues of how to express our personal preferences, which then leads to what side-effects, created by which system of providing our end-goal. These

Attractive delusion

available choices are a collective choice, with some governmental input usually. If we didn't pay for them, there wouldn't be lots of cars, is still true. This doesn't stop the feeling of the enormity of the power of the herd though. It's hard to swim against the current, which in these areas is feasible, the unfortunate situation being, that the existence of the 'norm' in the start and finish of these things happening the way they do, bring about the pollution that they do.

If I rent a flat from a landlord that has left the property insulated no better than it was over one hundred years ago, my choice is normally to have the heating on or not. My choice of utility bill providers, does give me some flexibility, though the bulk of the decision making is not in my control. Transport is a bit different, because I vote with my feet. In this case I am part of a herd, but have a range of methods of transport, and if wealthy enough, can even choose which colour it is. Here again we have a societal theatre. The path of both home heating and transport have not here been discussed with the extra pollution 'variable' involved. Having a large Victorian house with single glazed windows and unnecessarily large cars, are symbolic of financial success and seen as desirable. Public transport is accessible, but not normally seen as an end-goal aspiration. These are societal aspirations, which cannot be changed at the individual level, even without the desire to add in another factor which does not easily fit in. The difficulties in shifting the direction away from the unnecessary erosion of life, are not predominantly technological, but psychological.

Having used the term 'herd' to try to clarify how non-explicit ideology moves in waves of unconscious consensus, I have hit upon a relatively familiar psychological platform. Whom it is that think they are in this herd, can vary however. I would, with an obvious sense of arrogance, prefer to think of myself as someone who can observe this mass movement from an objective watchtower. But there are many others who consider themselves as above this mass of people, not as commentators but as superior beings who are not as gullible. We are comfortable explaining to each other how an ignorant mindset is the driving force behind the direction of society, so long as we are allowed to be seen as someone who is capable of rational analysis of this, and is no more than complicit in its' tolerance. 'That's just what is happening', is a form of agreement, so long as the individual commenting on this is seen as being capable of being on higher ground. This superiority can be political, economic or intellectual. Some people are pulling the strings that make the system operate more than others, and these 'powers that be' respect the herd as something they think they are guiding for their own good, bringing some responsibility, but not from entirely self-interest. This segregation of people, by those who think they can provide a service to humanity by keeping a mass of delusions content, and those who lack the ability to be involved in their own path, is intrinsically derogatory. Justification for conceptualising society as being made up of some slightly less capable cattle, can be from the economic standpoint of this being the mechanics of the system in operation. This is true, as in, this is the state of affairs in front of us. There are different viewpoints from which we can colour this analysis. What is interesting, is the different applications different people put the concept to. At one extreme, the concept of cultural, societal movement, can be seen as a quantum of data, a scale with which to categorize the thing we are describing. In a completely different manner, the concept of a cultural ideology being expressed on mass, can be seen as a moral justification for the principle behind it. It is important to keep the decision to approve of activities due to their popularity, very separate from the feeling of being part of an unstoppable tide without having any say in it. 'That's the way it is' is a deceivingly easy way to describe both.

A point of judgment worth noting, is that those who can frame themselves as being separate in the decision making department, from the mass movement into the affordable mess, are usually more than happy to see themselves as gaining from this momentum. This is an unconscious negotiation with their conscience. 'Benefit and no blame', would be a good summary. If the whole herd happens to be going somewhere, so be it, and in that I can enjoy the perks without showing any approval of the choice to go that way, which makes me a nicely paid bystander.

Starting with the negative expression of the 'herd' to describe the general population, adding a quizzical tone of why this mass of people are maintaining the demand side of the supply chain of goods and services leading to the probable next phase of unnecessary damage, meets with a variety of responses. A simple way to categorize these is to divide them into the ones which think the operating system behind this populist trajectory is working ok, and those who believe it is not.

Taking stock of the navigational heading, some people share their view that things are not good, but that the force of the flow of the populous has determined this outcome. This can be seen by the individual, as something which makes them a reluctant passenger of this wave. In this way they do not approve of the ethical outcome, but are powerless to change these mechanics. The same but with a different conclusion, is to have respect for the machine. This is to agree that the outcome is dubious, and that as an individual we have little sway in the general swing, but that we have 'opted in' for this democratic free movement of choices and have to respect the outcome. Both of these views are more of the position of an observer than a controller, one showing some regret in the results of the operating system, and the other with more of a feeling of collective collusion in our faith in freedom.

A more derogatory form of observation, is to see the results as those needed to keep the lesser equals in a state of satisfaction. From the position of believing that they have the ability to show more control over the outcomes in a favourable direction, these people believe they are constrained to keep the things as they are, and not rock the boat of the masses, in order to maintain their contentment, which requires the course of action to be doing nothing and showing no disapproval. Again, this is a form of faith in the operating system. The negatives of the way things are going can be observed by our superiors, and in theory could be controlled better, but the preference is to keep things going the way they are. The interesting point, is that we have three negative standpoints; a tidal wave of reluctant damage, a bad result from a decent machine, and the need to humour a harmful herd. An uncomplicated and logical reaction, would be to see how the operating system could be redirected. At a rough guess, I would say that this response would be less than one in a hundred people. How do we make things better? That is not an anxious inquisitiveness, but a logical response to failures in the system. 'That's just the way things are, there's nothing we can do about it', is the power of unconscious majority rule to stay in the status-quo. This is a passive reaction and hard to counteract. Due to the scale of the many diverse elements that are the literal instigation of this general direction, the opposing force would be a change of mindset, to maintain a new factor of consideration into virtually everything. This is an internal debate over whether to bother doing something or not, with the doing side taking extra effort without any great short-term materialistic benefits. The alternative strategy of resisting the negative outcomes of the current operating system, would be to avoid this personal effort and allow government powers to legislate on what is deemed reasonable and what is not. This again, on the scale of the individual is passive, but at the price of giving away some of their supposed control which is otherwise in the invisible hand.

We have quite a mixed and diverse way of analysing or identifying, for our own purposes, what we consider the general modern current to be, and formed by whom. An interesting point is how as individuals there is more than one way in this mix to consider ourselves to be powerless and superior at the same time. To pat yourself on the back as you recognize that things are in general going wrong, is a self-satisfying cover on a 'not going to bother' strategy. Fortunately, this lack of any real, credible positivity, is something which might prove harder to hide as things become clearer in how tolerating us digging our own graves, weather you think this is under your own leadership or not, is plain daft.

Attractive delusion

Attractive delusion

Attractive delusion

PERSONAL VERSUS SOCIAL RESPONSIBILITY

Social responsibility is an arena of collective results. In this realm the individual has an input, and is on the receiving end of a communal result. How large a group we consider to be social can vary. This could be a group of friends or an entire continent. How much power we have as a decision maker in this collective field of consequences varies between the situations and the individual. We have two slightly different elements in this same label, as social responsibility has a very real part of being the consequences ones' actions have on the communal welfare around you, in addition to which, social responsibility is a part of how your identity is made up, by your own and others perception of whether you are the kind of person to be concerned by things that matter or not. This is a bit of a coarse division we are making here, between the things we are actually responsible for, and the things people think we are responsible for. There are many levels of misinterpretation here, such as by being misunderstood by ourselves as to what we actually cause and things we think we do. In addition to this we may accidentally or deliberately misguide others perceptions. This is a good distinction though, as here we have a good recognition of the two sides of this particular coin, one being tangible and objective, the other being personal, social and psychological. How social responsibility presents itself to ourselves and others, varies according to meaning and interpretation. Even a diligent, materialist analysis of the real 'causes and effect' chain of events needs parameters and context.

Social identity is however, a very powerful motivator, with a variable range of interactions. Part of this is definitely responsibility. How we perceive others 'take' on us, as playing a responsible part of actions, versus a selfish role, is a defining point of our identity. A considerable amount of this being an unconscious perception of how we think others see us, not directly how we actually are when given time to introspectively analyse ourselves.

Personal responsibility must in some way differ from social responsibility. This can easily be clarified by the end points of consequences. As the personal realm of responsibility obviously faces inwards, the social responsibility is an interaction of the personal with the more collective field of results. The western ideology of individualism, very much carries the personal principle with it, the personal responsibility being the source of 'self-made' success. Attributions of the person, are seen as the dominant feature of accomplishment, outweighing circumstantial luck and competitive advantage from happenstance. The focal point being singular, not a collective sub-set, or group identity.

In some way the ideas of social identity in terms of success, and personal responsibility, are kept in different spaces in our mindsets to social responsibility. To be a good player in the field of achieving the desirable goals of financial comfort and consumer availability of great things, usually means you have done well in the path of personal fulfilment; solidifying your personal identity and achievement without crossing the line of unacceptable social inconsiderateness. The idea of a bad person in the context of social responsibility, means this variable has been brought in as a signifier, that is not usually present. Normally in this context, we play by the rules, that is all. How we are judged, and how we believe we are being judged, which form our sense of identity, is at very least in the commercial and consumerist world, about our ability to achieve through our attributions to get what we want, under the rules of the endeavour we are taking part in. The idea of considerateness, or social responsibility, is only brought in if we deviate from the accepted boundaries of behaviour, for example insider-trading or back-handers. So our effectiveness as a responsible person is rarely in a combined calculation with our effectiveness as an achiever in the individualist field of play. This would happen in a contradictory way. If we have made great success, but through breaking the rules of responsibility, this would then not be seen as true achievement, as it deviated from the normal cultural parameters.

As we have seen, sometimes our aspirations are actually moulded by our interaction with the rest of society. Our self-identity is not only how we think we will be interpreted in what we have got to be so far, but also what things we project ourselves towards, which involves, at least to some degree, a collusion or vibe, that is made up at the social level. This is very noticeable when the collective environment has taken a swing in a noticeable direction. This can be something physical and dramatic, but can also be something effective politically, economically and sociologically. Economic recessions bring a very clear change in confidence and happiness, which, through our sense of identity, influence the directions we would put our efforts towards. We are unlikely to look for ways to keep the world on the path of creative expression and happiness, when we feel economically insecure. We put this agenda on the back burner, with lots of explanatory thoughts such as 'nothing we can do'. Our mental agility and sense of identity closes down in the absence of this security. Xenophobia and suspicion come out, along with conservatism in a coping form, which tries to keep things simple. The concept of how as a society we collectively stop emphasising creative solutions to develop beyond our current situation, and instead try to reinforce a more simplistic, mechanistic 'do or die' survivalist strategy, can be observed in what happens. But this not only shows how we move in a collective direction, it shows how as individuals, our sense of identity, in terms of what things we are trying to target, get changed by the social environment. This has a determining influence on our sense of responsibility, in that the boundaries of what can be expected of us change.

For a short period of time, before the latest recession in the UK, there were two things that now seem to be highly unlikely to seem appropriate now. Solar panels for some people at one time, had a desirability of having managed to obtain the kit for obtaining future rewards, by being a personal investor in the future. This was seen as being brought about by their own financial and adaptive ability to find a positive application of their efforts. Nothing was being taken away from this person by a dark cloud of doom and despair. Their steps were in a good direction, upon a platform available to them from other achievements. It was an additional feature of their life they took pride and joy in, with both a belief that it made the world a better place, and the idea that in the long-term they would be better off from it too. This ideology is a lot less apparent now, as the main exposure the subject gets in the media is that there is a belief that the government has previously made the technology over-subsidised. The 'can-do' positive action, has been replaced by dismissive rebut of a burdensome fad. This activity can be seen in different ways dependent on a collective frame of mind, not just judging, but casting a general format of response into which we frame any independent thinking. When the concept of adaptive technology is new and exiting, in an era of economic security, there is a psychological accompaniment of forward looking, projectivism. This very same activity in a time of trying to cut back on unnecessary cost and effort, is accompanied with a psychological self-defence of trying to keep it out of the way of more primary concerns of security. Here we see that social responsibility at one stage, was seen to be an additional bonus of a personal project, moving in the right direction. Now, the same activity feels to have no bonus feature to anyone. The planet should still feel a bit positive towards it, but other than the manufacturer or owner, as a society we do seem to point a negatively tainted finger at it; which is not the same as being indifferent or ignoring it, as this is a true swing in direction of the generalised social format.

A very short episode, was when in the UK, the leader of the Conservative party flew to Norway to pose with some huskies, to show a party slogan of 'go green, vote blue' as an agenda. This was before the global economic crunch. There was a level of prosperity and security that made the additional feature of enjoying ourselves without creating unnecessary harm to the future, a 'variable', one of the leading parties didn't want to miss out on. Things are in a very different place now, where this variable seems very much expendable, as the nuts and bolts of getting money and stuff, must take precedence, and the luxury item of caring about the future can wait. For a while, you could show off about your super-insulated renewable energy home, in a way that was able to out-bling the old-fashioned 'it costs more to run' properties, in a new way that completely re-identified success. Myself, and other people who love solar panels, still exist, and haven't changed that much. But the dynamic of society and social identity has. Creative, positive solutions come out at times of comfort and security, the solar boys toys come out in a time of economic prosperity.

The above examples show an example of when social responsibility in some areas was accepted and accessible. In the subject area of climate change this doesn't happen very often. One good example of how responses can change, but the driver in the decision machine tends to stick to the programme, is the concept of what can be called 'mother nature'. In the early nineties when the climate problem appeared to be putting restrictions on the industrialised procession, the concept of technological solutions became desired as a fixer. This was in contrast to the concept of the 'not to be tampered with' mother nature. Here we had two opposing strategies of dealing with the problem, if it was accepted that something should be done. The technical fix, means our interaction with the climate can be dealt with by modifying our industrialisation process. The mother nature diplomats would rather we modify and reduce our impact, by respecting the constraint that is being demonstrated as needed by natural forces. The industrialists think we have the power to keep control through modification, the nature people think we would be overpowered by our inability to take heed. Thirty years later, things are very different. Anybody who cared in either way has been shown that very little other than an acceleration of doom has been achieved. A technical remedy, or any means of sharing the concept of reducing the damage as socially acceptable, would be great. Here's the irony though. Those with the least desire to have anything done, are now like nature lovers, citing the power of nature to make any remedial action insignificant - volcanoes, dinosaurs anything at hand to show how mother nature does her own thing and we must just carry on as we are. Responsibility has moved from having trust in technology to remove the need to restrict any activity, to showing trust in nature to make any inability of technological cures to fix the problem, of no concern. The economic driver of industrial processes will not be impeded by new parameters of pollution. To say that these contrasting judgments are made by exactly the same people thirty years apart, is a bit of a rough guess, but I think a good one. Either way, it can be seen how responsibility is not a fixed hallmark. The cut of someone's jib may not change, whilst different flags are flown under different circumstances and ages.

Here's an example of how the core of moral responsibility held by someone, is not always shown by the statements made by that person. Flat-earthers of various kinds, show an emotional commitment to not opening the doors to the possibility of accepting climate change as part of reality. Part of this is usually the desire to carry on as they are, which is in a part 'selfishness' outranking consideration, another part of this does however come from morality. Unconsciously, the flat-earther has made an analysis of the probable programme of works, which would follow from the flip-side of their preferred non-reality track. This comes to a swift conclusion by their own adequate moral deliberation, that large amounts of things should be undertaken to respond to the conundrum. This imposing reconsideration of the status-quo, is the motivation to nip this annoyance in the bud. Thus follows a twist to reality, along with the help of large numbers of people and media, to reinforce this stance. As terrible as this may be, the inner sense of responsibility of these people is actually sound. These people have not taken a cold, calm moment of deliberation on how much to care about the situation. They have unconsciously responded with a knee-jerk they find hard to reverse.

The flat-earthers don't have an application of social responsibility towards the climate, but neither do most people, in most of society, for the majority of the time. Why is this? As came up earlier, the way we see ourselves as presented to others, as responsible or not, does in some way differ from the way our actions have good or bad consequences in the real world. This divergence between perception and actuality exists, at the collective as well as the individual level. Which decisions we make that are deemed by society as those which should take serious consideration, are judgments that have a signifier of importance. In the other direction, so do other things which are given a free reign, being labelled as not having any moral bearing attached to them. This is a natural and helpful way for a society to work. Each of these actions then does not need a cost-benefit investigation. The collective, psychological labelling system, may not be as accurate as a life-cycle spreadsheet, but a lot quicker and in the need of hardly any mental energy. In this way societal 'norms' of practice, help things run smoothly. In modern western society, individualism and consumerism have influenced this area to a great extent. These features have two combined influences on our collective mental platforms.

As an individualist, the way we end up, is to the greatest extent, down to what we make of ourselves. The critical input into the outcome, is the efforts and energy we apply, given the fixed building blocks of life we have in our toolbox. In a materialist culture, much of my success in this field will be displayed in physical objects. In a consumerist society however, the decisions on which things these are, is based to the greatest extent, on whether I want them and can afford them. Any complications to the process of desire and attainment are of little significance. This playground is obviously attractive to those who can feel free to express their branding, with trophies of happiness and luxury items, without burdensome thinking. Somewhat ironically though, this paradigm of individualism and uncomplicated consumerism, is also attractive to those who have not ended up so well equipped. Aspirations come from somewhere. We share the market place, and this is unconsciously kept simple, including for the desires of people who don't have very much. There are packaging claims of 'this and that' sustainability aspects, some of which are hard to believe. The noticeable feature of consumer psychology though, is that anything related to the suitability of the item being available, unconsciously by the individuals, is deemed as having been dealt with before it hit the market, making any further thought on this matter unnecessary. Those who have, and those that do not, have the future held open for them by their aspirations and desires, they can see the goalposts presented by the market. The side-effect of this though, is that our ability to feel connected with the consequences of our decisions, other than as a purchaser of things, becomes diminished. We feel no responsibility for the chain of events that follows from us wanting stuff that is available. Responsibility only comes into our minds, when brought in, usually in a social exchange, as having stirred something up, having enlivened an Ooooh. Most of the time, responsibility has gone to sleep, directly as a consequence of a simplistic operating system based on individualistic desire in a consumer based field. Gossip and procrastination bring a moral variable out for discussion, which, when getting on with life and wanting or needing things, is not usually there.

The idea of collective responsibility for a planetary concern has been in and out of the conscious attention of society. But on the whole, more so now than before, as it has gone around the block a couple of times, it is not at the table. One of the main reasons for this, is its' incompatibility with the easy to handle mindset of individualistic consumerism. The power of this way of thinking comes from the independent nature of social responsibility, psychologically, from the real world consequences. Under this paradigm, most of the time, responsibility can be kept asleep, and the goals kept in sight. This is for both the 'haves' and the 'have nots'. Without the poor to contrast themselves with, using adornment of great expense and limited availability, the wealthy would be lost. Just by being there, not to everyone, but to a lot of the less lucky people, the over indulgent provide a simple format of aspiration. Wanting to have a lot of money is not daft, but along with this usually comes a popular appendage of materialist consumerism with no consideration for other people or the planet. Wealthy people actually need this desire, which other people have, to stay on track. If the damage done by being rich and inconsiderate were more noticeable, and stood out from the desires of the general population to live a communal sustainable existence, they would be off a risk-free pedestal created by a collective desire to have things that good. This may sound like an extremist soundbite, but it turns out that in general, wealthy people pollute more than the less wealthy, just because they can. This is not definitive, but true, both when comparing people with each other in their country of residence, or contrasting all occupants of different countries of varied wealth. This should not lead to a conclusion that we should become communist and live in identical blocks of flats all around the world. The observation of this part of reality, is more interesting in what the perspectives in our mental make-up are reflections of. The world is a communal place, the result here being inevitable, as pollution in particular is trans-boundary. The problem we have mentally, is that it is hard, even in the back of our minds, to aspire to have all the objects and availabilities of the blindly inconsiderate wealthy, and at the same time be critical of any unnecessary harm brought about by this. The main reason for this, is the way planetary concern could be a pervasive complication to almost every decision. If let into the judgment zone, this calculation process contradicts the consumerist *tabular raza* operating system, which allows individualism to 'go get' with the other half of the brain unoccupied.

With the intention of showing how life could be lived without causing so much trouble for others by taking time to look at production processes and sources of material, ie information about the provision of a product, the psychological response of myself and usually everyone else, is the feeling that a hint of doom has come into play, albeit on the side of making things not so bad. This kind of emotion is what is expected when an additional requirement is placed upon you, for example, when you receive what someone said they would give you, but then they add a 'could you just'. That's an easy way to spoil a favour, as things were going without any further requirements, then the flow was interrupted. This is not always the case, but is a reasonably accurate analogy of how an attachment of environmental concern would be felt to a normal consumerist chain of thought. If we look at this from the other way around though, in a consumer decision, this doesn't make it Ok to ignore a sweatshop maltreatment of workers, or the loss of rainforest for a hamburger, nor would most people consciously make that prognosis. The main problem with environmentally friendly thinking, which is actively dissuasive subconsciously, is that when you take an interest in looking into the chain of events where this is relevant, there is very little which will go untouched. The typical conclusions to conscientious thoughts of these kinds, is restrictive in the parameters of what would be deemed acceptable or not. We can see therefore, the attractiveness of any processes, which would relieve us of this hindrance to an easier motivational programme. The conclusion, can be a simple 'don't have this, have that' exchange of alternatives, but this is a result of deliberation, mentally requiring effort, not a switch with no input.

When you put yourself within the connectedness of reality, most things matter. What is apparent in a positive nature though, is that the critical catalyst to this brainstorming, other than being considerate about the future, is information. How much of this we can handle, or choose to ignore, including a new plateau of interpretation, is the modern worlds' bread and butter. Reality is accessible, along with a lot of other stuff in the information age, and if we engage our minds in response to the consequences actions will have, this should form a dialogue of the future unfolding. The comparative results of considerateness versus disengagement, should be a social platform of awareness. Being 'greener than thou' can happen and be annoying. But that is a burden I don't think will come up very often, which if compared to maintaining a delusion that things are going Ok, when they definitely are not, is not that bad.

What has become quite apparent, is that what we would normally call morality, which considers differing attitudes to responsibility, rarely goes through, or even can't get through, many psychological processes barriers. This causes emotional responses and a difficulty in then clearing the air for some rational appraisal resembling an ethical discussion. If we were to revert to what is commonly understood as what morality actually is, what would be the great hinge-points of judgments? In this very diverse field of judgment, it is best to try and pick out the most salient features of this particular area of applied ethics. Harm being causally connected to individuals choices, is one thing, along with the difference ethically between the intended and unintended consequences. An additional perspective is the theory of rights, or the liberty of individuals, this being a discussion on both freedom from harm from others and freedom to do things of your own volition. If harm is being caused, and this is avoidable at no great cost, this would normally be deemed as an undesirable action from a basic utilitarian perspective. A different moral perspective is the principle of a social contract, where codes of conduct are determined by a collaborative agreement. What we have here is three very rough, differing foundations for ethical principles. One is a simple cost-benefit programme, which can come in many different versions. A second is the idea that principles are set in 'categorical imperatives' of 'thou shall not' and similar, which are set in the nearest thing a philosopher can find to resemble stone. The third is based upon rules and codes, which are man-made agreements and therefore more variable than truths of the universe such as a Pythagoras equation, but are not a simple matter of choice of individuals independently.

The cost-benefit approach to moral judgments can be the deliberation over the consequences to actions, these being not necessarily restricted to just material things. Peoples' feelings as well as physical objects can be furthered or hindered by choices we make. The point here worth looking into, is that, in and of itself, this principle opens up the debate of at what level of hindrance or burden would the 'at no great cost' be considered to have been crossed. What costs should we be willing to pay for what benefit, where? If we restrict humans to be the only receivers or losers in this calculation, other forms of life not being counted as having any intrinsic value, how would this be further demarcated in terms of importance based on distance in space and time, and familiarity of these to the agent causing the consequences? At some level of delay in the cause and effect scenario, the consequent becomes seen as happenstance, not only in a natural way to not make the connections, but also in the separateness of being judged on the consequence and the doing of the deed. However, if we continue to create pollution without massive changes to the quantities of this very quickly, the world is going to get messy, with a lot of suffering now and in the future. 'How much pollution should we morally be allowed to cause now without any feeling of guilt', would be a simple cost-benefit response. What are the benefits to the individual, and what are the costs in the short and long-term? This is not an easy calculation, but the principles, which should be apparent to anyone with a basic understanding of moral worth, are easily understood and debated if the desire is there, which it seems, for most of us, is at the moment unfortunately rare.

Deontic, including rights theory, may, as it comes from a different type of judgment, nullify some cost-benefit calculations, as some people believe that some principles are there regardless of the outcome. This can go either way, in making decisions in the environmental field more hard-line or less so. The discussion to be had on this is over what is the language of interpretation of the main drivers. For example, a simple 'do unto others' as a principle, can have a massive range of disagreement over range of application in space, time and species. But the easy conclusion to draw from any moral discussion on the subject, is that the debate, even if in disagreement, is on what effort should be made, by what people, where and when. This principle of a moral imperative, can counteract consequentialist calculations by not accepting a variation from a code of conduct. For example, steeling something from someone in order to prevent them then following on to create harm to a greater number of people, may be seen as not being feasible, due to the lack of adherence to the principle of never stealing. The opinion that the subject is best ignored, is rarely the result of discussion over morality or responsibility, no matter how tricky it is to see what lines should or should not be crossed. Here, in the arena of rights, we would also have discussions over the liberty of individuals, who have the right to make choices for themselves, without having moral codes impinged upon them by those who feel they know better. These can be great debates, carving out what principles we think should be the foundations for a future we are determining by our actions now, and what level of freedom we have in this theatre.

The concept of there being a social agreement of basic rules, upon which we all must base our guidelines, can open an interesting box. If there is a social contract, how do we define who are the participants? Does this somehow get intuitively communicated across the globe in different cultural perspectives? Are people not born yet, brought into the contractual benefits, or are they, along with other minorities who perhaps would prefer not to participate at all, given some discounted leverage?

What is evident from any of these perspectives, is that there is in most peoples' interpretation, some form of civic duty, or obligation, to apply concepts derived from more than pure self-interest. Some principles may be defined as concrete, but this would be a deviation from the idea that there is a range of decisions and behaviours which are sometimes more and sometimes less permissible. Deontology is the moral philosophy with the rules set in a rational code from deduction. In comparison to the consequential sums, this often makes for a more definitive 'is or isn't' on, or off decision procedure. This kind of thinking however, may have more susceptibility to far-off long-range consequences not being included in the moral judgment process. It is not uncommon to have the idea that causing pain in others is not morally sound, but to carry this moral code within yourself is very easy to do whilst accidentally putting another straw on an important camels' back. Certain levels of conspicuousness are needed for everyday thinking to be alerted to the crossing of a moral line.

Another interesting point in the debate on the morality over climate change and the population movements following from this, is that if this were to be taken seriously, and we were to look for the remedy, what are the costs to be paid for this realignment? Purely as a philosophy and psychology discussion over the ethics of this, we can see the differing types of influence between the primary and secondary emotional desires. If there are things we have to go without in order to keep things on track for a sustainable future, there are some things, which are rarely considered as reasonable to ask people to sacrifice, such as basic nutrition, water, or some form of shelter. Whereas, other things are seen as pandering to more unnecessary emotional goals, or are things which gains their status from being seen by others as well as oneself as being luxurious. This is a simple debate over what things may be in the ingredients of what people get and what results this leads to, both scientifically in terms of the state of the planet, and emotionally, in terms of how we see ourselves on the ladder of gaining desirable things in the culture we are surrounded by. This form of deliberation, so far, has for mostly psychological reasons, not really appeared in western society. As mentioned before, it is this cost-benefit conundrum, which makes innovative solutions in providing things at a lower environmental cost, rationally desirable. If the reason we are currently indifferent to how things are going in this field, is that we have come to this conclusion after giving it consideration, then why does this discussion never come up?

Attractive delusion

Attractive delusion

There are lots of things propping up the shape of the desired form

PARADIGM MAINTENANCE OR PARADIGM SHIFT

Insert chapter eight text here. Insert   Some things are more likely to keep things on their current track than others. Shifts in paradigm can take quite an upheaval to be tolerated, as the 'out' of the box is what is needed to turn things around. Here is where we can contrast the difference between a complete rejection of an ideology, with a new way of mixing information in the existing system. The idea of legislative control being given more powers to influence what choices we can make in a previously free arena, is not going to be met with anything other than derision. Even when the patterns of cost and benefit are calculated, psychological mindsets will conjure and bend things into ridicule. People of older generations have made the transition from a mixed economy with more simplistic government and legislative control, to the more free-market, liberating the individual and companies to make transactions in the market place. As we have mentioned, this has brought great benefits. Additional variables that were in their time not around, are not going to be easily let into a previously capable sphere. These people have witnessed liberation and a new mindset develop, where success was becoming more attached to the effort put in by the individual rather than a coat of family arms, or boys club connections. These people of older generations, who witnessed this change in cultural structure, share society with the rest of us. Our thoughts and perspectives blend in with each other in a society, so shifting quickly is hard to motivate. Having any limits on the amount of pollution caused by a country is quite a new concept, which jars against the wishes to produce things quickly and efficiently if you have seen things, including your own freedom, become more available through this industrial and economic process. As the collective cultural paradigm is created and maintained, mostly unconsciously, to a large degree by people happy with or trying to succeed in the status quo, the changeability of this is slow and needs something to be quite significant to change its' direction.

In a completely different way to having a restriction on activities, which is understandably perceived to be the central motto of the environmental paradigm, is the new freedom of information brought about by technological changes. It is a lot easier to find out about a lot of things. Sometimes in a messy, inaccurate way, but we are all aware of the huge shift in the arrival of an information age.

Our ability to be able to trigger a greater level of thinking, quite literally more insightful, rather than an inhibition to find out what is going on behind the scenes in the provision of things, would be acceptable and influential. This in some way could be seen as trying to motivate disruption, which is not positive. The principle here though, could be to clarify reality. We don't all want to dig around for mud to sling. But the process of gaining information can also be on the positive side. Beyond the delusive strategy of advertising, some companies take extra efforts to be open and honest in a good light about themselves. These companies with minimum wage policies and sustainability principles, are surviving in a commercial world with honesty not being the sales pitch, just a reality in addition to economic effectiveness. Here they have a motivation to show an ideological format of their production, which, without compromising their effectiveness, can coincide with their self–interest. Things do not always make this likely, but it does show these factors are not necessarily completely co-joined. Mostly, this additional factor is not there in the market place activities of us free consumers. Without a psychological shift in caring about the planet, we are not going to find information about the feed-back loops of various consumerables, or unnecessary damage caused by production processes, interesting. However, for those of us who are concerned about this, or other matters, the system of the consumerism, marketing, sales and production, can quite easily be just as it is already, with a small addition of gossip and information giving us preferences, or hindrances to indulgence, that can change the sense of involvement in what it is we support in the market place.

The small scale individual choice process can be enhanced by collecting, sharing and discussing information. But at a more interesting level, the same thing can be done about the planet. Where are people going to be displaced from? From what countries can we expect migration as a consequence of sea-level changes? As droughts become more severe and their locations shift, where and for what number of people can we expect crop failures? What parts of the world are going to produce the things we currently like to consume? There are going to be large shifts in people, temperature and stuff. But what is very uncommon, and certainly shouldn't be for younger generations who are going to be living through these transitions, is a clear discussion of these events and their outcomes. Along with starvation, the loss of life from migration attempts, conflict over scarce resources, are not going to go away. The developed world is responsible for the outcomes about to unfold, to a large extent in the unintended side effects of carbon emissions. In the west, we still depend on things being brought from all around the world. Unfortunately, psychology has another part to play in how we picture the world around us.

'Us and them' is a simple demarcation. This, despite the negativity associated with this phrase, is used in our unconscious cognitive assimilation of the large-scale picture around us. Our zones of effectiveness and involvement are natural mental boundaries we need to conceptualise with in a pattern of description. If a country a long way away has extreme difficulties, we can assist them. This goes through the stages of seeing they need help, and our framing ourselves as being responsible, considerate, collective societies who can offer help. Sometimes this is followed with aid, and sometimes with 'pledges' to provide something later on, probably. If this started the other way round, with our feeling irresponsible for creating the mess, and the help we can provide being a small part of making up for the suffering we have caused, our responses would be psychologically very different, even if the help given were exactly the same. Giving the same amount of help feels very different if you feel you are being told to do so, by yourself or others, versus stepping up to a generosity, helping hand, integrity plate. This is a very brash and simplistic abbreviation of the current and forthcoming world. However, this is the point. The biggest boundary to assessing the cost-benefit of the future, is as a society which has an inhibition to admitting to having had made mistakes, to such an extent that change is seen as untenable as it is intrinsically connected with blame by the causal links. The opposite if this would be to accept change as pioneers, or innovators at the head of the field. In both of these scenarios however, there is an 'us and them' mental division, which is necessary for us to calibrate collective action.

With information transfer and honesty, we can see where the world is going. If the next generation of people heading into working society, running jobs and making spending power decisions, do not have the faintest idea of the path their predecessors have set them on, they cannot be expected to make difficult decisions. As important as removing ignorance, is our ability emotionally and psychologically to live in a world that is not made to tick-over on delusion. The future is an open book.

An honest strategy as a nation, to declare that we are aware of the difficulties, but don't care, is very hard to announce. Keeping our awareness of reality asleep, and clouding over any disruptive complications with sociological mindsets focused on self-interest, is a lot easier. Information and discussion, not government forced legislation, could be the step-change needed to bring us back to a reality involved in the real world, part of which can be fun, love and appreciation for people and things all over the globe. Once the majority of the public have a care, or an interest in something, governments can make adjustments, or large scale policy changes. Legislation can come after we have made our minds up in a free way. If, unlike this, the psychological feel of a thing is that it is a hindrance, its' instigation is more like a dictatorship. Having things the other way round, of people thinking first, does provide a sense of belonging and involvement, which I think, used to be around a lot more.

As reality unfolds, which is happening in weather patterns, droughts and floods, the ease of delusion will diminish. Honesty and information will, I hope be available. But the way things are framed in our thinking will, if it is to support the current unrealistic system, need to have increasingly strong paradigm maintenance. The strategy of admitting responsibility at the same time increasing the barriers to migration, would only be possible if morality were to be announced as a luxury. To literally have geographical boundaries to consideration, as a principle that can be worn on one's sleeve, would be to show that humans have evolved into things as emotionally advanced as mammals, creating unnecessary damage and then pulling up the drawbridge to those who suffer the most from it. Pride in one's home country is normal, but the boundary that would be needed here, is that beyond that, one doesn't care 'at all', which is very different from the usual more dignified 'prioritising'. This is difficult to take any joy in picturing, but is a simple analysis of the most likely direction the world is taking; thus comes the attractiveness of any delusion which will take this away and help me focus on helping everyone else by not bothering to think about it and going shopping. Reality and honesty can be a tough pill to take, meaning the motivation to keep the veil of honour alive with lies, will persist despite the increasing availability of factual and scientific analysis.

What I am trying to show is the depth and possible advantage, of what would in its very nature, be a paradigm shift. The change is in perspective not specifics. A technique for succeeding in progress, at the personal level, is to question oneself, to add a bit of doubt, in a kind of 'I could have improved slightly by doing it more..'. This is a psychological removal of complacency, bringing fine-tuning, or adaptation, making room for improvement in the mindset. At the production level at work, this is very much there, and encouraged to bring efficiency. In our consumer based ideology however, this is not available. The simple desire or want of having or doing something is a motivational driver, and will not take interference. It could be thought of as something that is mostly directionally fixed, which is either going that way or it is not. Its' not that unthinkable that imagination and creativity are still alive, so where has moral care and inquisitiveness had to go? As seen earlier, some of these desires can be fulfilled in slightly different ways, to the same effect, without the consequential damage. All that is needed is awareness and a bit of considerate thinking. By being aware that the normal mindset of people in our society is dumbed down by the psychological infrastructure of the invisible hand of consumerism, can bring a sense of well-being to the individual, if your willing to engage in a more emotionally developed strategy - of bothering to think beyond your own immediate wishes. This is not for everyone, nor anyone all the time. Having an approach however, of seeing the positive mark of not competing for just 'getting and having' at the exclusion of more civilised endeavours, does bring some self-esteem.

What is very noticeable when some current mild forms of conscientiousness is displayed by manufacturers, is that in a lot of cases where some form of responsibility has been declared, the people consuming these things will not appear very effected by this change. Its' more like an unrelated appendage of little interest, emotionally of little significance. When the best result available feels as if it is some form of add-on showing consideration at some level, like a token or logo, this is an additional feature to co-exist with the after affect of the unchanged desire transaction. The idea of information being ready available, such as corporate social responsibility about things which are out there is great, but there is not really enough room on the packaging to describe in a meaningful way the global sequence of events, meaning with most people, the feeling is that this is purely greenwash, and not a shift in *modus operandi*.

This shows why it is the paradigm which is a more serious

element, which comes from *within* at the outset. The current operating system which will not change in direction, usually bringing an unconscious, unintended lack of care with it, whether a badge of dignity is added or not. Wiping out the free-market is not the required antidote, nor is adding a swathe of red-tape, just a recognition of the value of thoughtfulness, which is not obligatory and can come and go at the whim of the individual along with any other feelings they are at liberty to have.

Some primary emotions, such as desire, are not made to be messed about with. When a core driver is in operation, such as anger, it is other tools in the box, which are needed to change the behavioural direction. It is therefore perfectly natural for a simplistic system for getting things and providing things to be preferred. What is noticeable is how this stretches beyond the core emotion, in suppressing our natural ability to have other feelings interact with our judgments. This is still in the area of motivational plan schematics though. Here we have the hinge point between shifting a paradigm, and the alternative of putting a smaller amount of mental effort, into maintaining the current mindset. This stretch from a quicker, more instant 'like it', to a more complicated interaction of different levels of thinking is similar to the difference between instant gratification and patience for greater, longer-term benefits. Some times of course, are better than others for this. When it comes to consumer ideology though, it is noticeable that the idea of following 'self-interest' as the main director of the operating system, as opposed to more diverse thinking frameworks, is an accurate analogy of how we psychologically develop morally. This is not the same thing as how market trade or simple transactions are supposed to happen though. This, in theory, is an unrelated subject to the moral integrity of anything. But unfortunately, environmentalism has invaded this field, not in everyone's mindset, but certainly in terms of how things in reality are related to each other. In this subject area, it is how things are a consequence of the choices and decisions we make, even when from the appearance and your initial feelings, it may not seem to have any connection with any outcomes other than whether you want it or not. It is from this perspective that discussion and information exchange can engage between people as to how they recognize different features of things. Interaction about the surrounding world and how this can change through what I think and say and do, is a complication, but liberating too. As it turns out that without knowing it, in our unconscious trust of the market system to make deliberation unnecessary through a sense of communal approval, we have actually given away our connectedness with control over what is around us. We are taking our social and shopping environment to be pre-determined through the efficiency and money programme, beyond any influence any of us can have. If something is available to us, that makes it at least morally tolerable. However outside of this mode of thought, if there is an awareness that something is bad, and should change, then this can be shouted about. Being responsible for the death and suffering of other people in the future, through the idea of showing your success as a person by owning and using an unnecessarily large 'powerful' car, whether aware of the chain of connection or not, is plain stupid. This pleasure is taken by thousands of people, glorifying themselves whilst either staying ignorant or dispensing with care. This can be made less popular purely in societal knowledge that these people are either stupid or deliberately extinguishing other peoples' lives. You don't have to stamp your feet or wave a placard, just talk to your friends and people around you and see what they think.

In the work 'The Measurement of moral judgment,' Colby and Kohlberg do make references to others, Piaget, Weber and Baldwin, who have also looked into the field of how we develop psychologically in our moral judgments. Of the six categories of 'type' they have assigned as stages, the first begins in childhood with an acceptance that some things are right and some things wrong, with being told, or told off, by usually the authority figures of parents, indicating to the individual that that's the way things are. This is a mental picture of rules that are as concrete as any of the ideas we learn about. After some time this develops into the idea that you and I may have wishes that conflict each other, and we hereby enter a slightly different realm of exchange and negotiation. My own desires have to be put into a deal making scenario where I have to see how to get for myself 'this' given that other people also have their own interests.

The third stage starts to construct what could be described as the beginnings of a moral sense, where the physical consequence of getting or not getting my way also involve the code of conduct of intention, which is a 'why' not just a 'what'. Here we have a principle that there are rules of engagement, which should be followed not purely to avoid being punished if caught, or as a bargaining platform. With this is the idea of moral principles having an objectively independent nature of what they are, over and above principles of exchange between individuals. These can be made by individuals in a surrounding society, but the principles reside in this common ether, not just in each person as and when they wish. The last two stages could be described as hard to define, as some people get as far as relativism and are happy with that, and other people have less of a 'socially constructed' perspective. Trying to define realism, or objectivism is a discussion, which has gone on for centuries.

The point I'm making though, is that although morality is hard to define, what can be easily seen, is that earlier on in our development of reasoning about things, there is the principle of simple exchange, followed by how some things are right or wrong beyond me and what I want. To accidentally steel something is not as wrong as deliberately steeling the same thing. This can then take on many different types of interpretation into a social contract, a cultural paradigm or even divine command.

I suggest, as an explanation of much of the damage causing 'mindsets' we seem to be stuck with, that the unbridled trust in the mental attributes of free-market exchange, which is based on a childlike early-stage understanding of following self-interest only, is culturally hindering. What the usual later stages of moral development do, is supervene this 'tit for tat' platform with a more complex senses of exchange, fairness and justice. The lack of need for this kind of deliberation over most market based activity, has made us less capable of activating this aspect of thinking.

The idea of the reason behind the use of Adam Smiths' invisible hand in the free-market, is a fairly complicated blend of ideas leading into a collective outcome, because the understanding leads to the application of a moral principle in justifying the socially engineered, market-force based platform. It is a theorem of guiding principles, breaking down intentions and interactions, into an equation leading to what are the preferred resulting circumstances. But the motivated individual 'agents' to be used as the building blocks of the theory, in the mind of the system designers, is 'homo economicus', which is not nearly as sophisticated as the programme itself. When taking part in the free-market, it is not supposed that the principle of the 'greater good' will come into anyone's thinking at all. It is the goal to achieve this collective success, but by the brilliant system of having activity self-regulated by self-interest, with no need for a more mature deliberation about the interaction. The bountiful outcome of having things work efficiently, is the ethical consequence motivated by the intention to increase happiness deliberately, by not needing individuals to try. This works very well, but it does come with a footnote declaring that this is not the best form of thinking for all things at all times. Nor does it suppose that any higher level of thinking made redundant in this exercise should therefore be turned off in the rest of our experiences.

The idea that something is judged as wrong by the individual, when the consequence has negative side effects coming back upon the individual themselves, and does not get judged so when it does not, is a form of early development associated with some people who are only troubled by criminal acts they commit, by the punishment they may endure, and only that aspect of the activity. Shown by some studies, is that the minds of some criminals who repeat their crimes, is that the realm of their thinking in terms of moral development, is not beyond the principle of avoiding being disciplined by diverging from externally given guidelines. The 'wrongness' is simply not there if not caught. This is a simple, but a reasonable analogy to individualistic consumerism, where the end-goals are limited purely to the inward looking process of gratification as a core driver, without any broader thinking into how some things exist as principles not directly related to personal feedback loops. This framework of judgment doesn't of itself constrict other thought patterns, but can be thought of as having some sort of appeal, as it runs a simple programme. Weight can come off the shoulders, if the mind can downsize the requirement to the same as that which can be done by people of early stages of development, leaving space in the mind for anything else, including relaxing or fun.

      Having been subsumed by the consistent application of this dumbing down of consideration, the next generations of people who will end up in charge of the direction of the worlds ideologies, often have an unexpectedly complicit mindset. Despite being more aware than people were before, of the way things are going, there is a noticeable 'have to accept the way things are' attitude. We don't however, have to accept the 'status quo', the belief that you do, being a great self-maintenance pattern for the existing operating system. Along with this is a general complacency that 'we're screwed', full stop. This is an unfortunately negative tinge with which to define normality, particularly as participation is a necessary aspect of the maintenance of this momentum. There is a lot of sense in knowing that bucking the system rarely leads to an easy life. When outnumbered and overpowered, the current of the stream is very strong. Many people have active minds though, and why should they accept doom and suffering as an inevitable consequence of their forefathers and their cohabitants being a bit crap? The world is still there and so are we. A whole planet of people can interact with greater ease than ever before, and discuss where things are going and what to do about it. It is this sense of being a part of the world in an active way, that could fill the 'future makers' with a sense of excitement and belonging. This is where there is a surprising amount of reticence in comparison to reactivism, showing the scale of the inertia in the current road map. There is currently a global recession, or global financial bodge. But as a species, we are not in a self-defining quagmire, unless we wish to continue to make one and make the decision to delude ourselves that this is all that is available. It is only a simple 'taking of stock' of the situation that brings a 'hang on a bit', which I hope, will become more noticeable and encourage the direction of our 'progress' to be questioned and changed.

Attractive delusion

STATE OF THE WORLD

What we have developed, is the analysis that there are different patterns with which to frame the state of the world. This makes psychological triggers of response vary in answers to questions about where we are now, where can we expect the world to be going, and for what reasons. As reality unfolds, an increasingly significant part of anyone's mind-set is how they connect the activities of humans and the state of the planet. Part of this is their cause and effect paradigm, another part being blame or responsibility. The first of these is a situational programme, on how to classify physical actions with consequences. The second however, is actually a social, moral and emotional response pattern. On these two fronts, beliefs will have to diverge more greatly in their explanations, as circumstance becomes increasingly apparent. Having clarified where a lot of these belief systems come from, and what they are reinforced by, we can contrast these views on in what ways they will become more stand-point based, and what ideas they will need to maintain themselves as conditions become more extreme.

The concept that climate change is not part of reality will become increasingly ridiculous. This doesn't stop the leader of the USA believing it, unfortunately, but that puts an interesting distinction on what it means to them, to hold that belief. Maintaining a delusion for convenience, brings a personal-identity feature to that person. In the individual, there is part of them not willing to go to that stage of adaptation, no matter what. This however, gives other people a beautifully simple stereotype with which to identify them – FlatEarther. There are drivers in the motivational systems of these people, which will not facilitate disruption to their existent framework, even by the truth. There is an appeal to the concept that no matter what people do, the planet creates its' own state of well-being, giving humans a complete freedom of choice in the playing field of life. This will lose credibility as the cause and effect of pollution lead to a more established sense of connectedness between human activity and the planets climate. If these people won't budge, how do they fit in a schematic of society trying to align itself with reality, within a country which negotiates with all other countries of the world on how much responsibility or action has to be taken in order to appear reasonably responsible in a fast changing world without taking too much of the burden? Unfortunately it seems as if this situation is in some ways already occurring. Flat-earthers are taking a standpoint on the cause and effect side of analysis, which is a simple empirical matter. But, as is clear, like responsibility and blame, this particular response is actually based on emotional and psychological triggers. Some members of society have delusional paradigms of judgment, and these are then being taken up in the mix, in a plethora of averaged out responsibility reduction. This is disappointing, as the sensible response to the particular standpoint of *non-reality* becoming increasingly ridiculous, is ridicule. How things move culturally however, are a very different shift in tides from this philosophical deliberation.

Nicknames and stereotypes are more likely to shift perceptions than analysis of psychological self-deception. For example, if a public spokesman known as having a laudable style of understanding, makes a declaration that climate change is fictional, has a greater influence on the general acceptance that this is foolish, when compared to the effectiveness of a simple, rational scientific publication clarifying the boundaries of reality. The hinge-point of these divergences being flagged up, is that the main body of the culture needs a coherent ground from which these delusional beliefs can be discredited. This is the difference between blending in a range of beliefs with each other, and coming to a binary point of 'is or isn't it' a good fit with the main cultural operating system. The question is whether society is going to move in this direction or not. For example, women have the vote, and slavery is wrong. Now we have a consensus on these simple principles being upheld, divergence from these are very conspicuous. Historically though, these ideas were not adhered to as common knowledge, and needed a transition into acceptance, at least by those benefiting from its' denial. At the moment in the West, the idea that pollution is a problem that needs addressing, is in the 'yeah, but..' box, which, if it doesn't become a more serious type of majority view, will not dispel the ability of flat-earth to stay in the mixing pot for a cultural generalisation of not bothering to change.

As made clear, part of the difficulties is in the lack of observable, direct causal connectedness in the invisible and time delayed consequences, unlike equal rights issues which show the after-effects much more up-front and noticeable. In the case of climate change and the resulting upheaval of sustainability for large numbers of people, there is need for a small amount of rational deliberation on what is unfolding, before the gut-wants, don't-likes, get out to compare themselves with the ones already there in consumerism. The feature of a culture is that there can be ridiculous stand-points, if the societies psychology will carry it.

Flat-earth, on the whole should be on the decline, but this does leave a huge middle ground of responsibility removal and hand-in-the-sanding. These dispositions are signals that the emotional drivers are still in the simplest strategy position compatible with individualistic consumerism. The game of showing who you can be identified as being, by the things you want and get through your own effort and skills, can still be the rules you play by, even in a world where pollution matters, so long as others accept that as well. That is why the transition is hard. Even when reality is accepted, the easiest way to succeed in the current programme is to make that not matter to you, in your individualist progress report. The less you know about it the better, and if notified of a chain of events you may be implicated in, point the finger somewhere else. Anyone showing concern for additional features in the competitive market place for success, will be at a natural disadvantage. So why would anyone volunteer for such a set-back? In this way there needs to be a common understanding that we can judge each other on. This means something not just on what we get and have, but that in caring about pollution and the resulting suffering of others, that makes us more of a dignified person.

Having a positive and constructive attitude after the onset of another flavour of doom is not impossible. If the table does turn, and the reality of the connectedness of human pollution and the planets temperature becomes general knowledge, personal choices and activities can still vary from great to rubbish, within this category of acceptance. Depending on the country one lives in, this can still vary in terms of individualistic competitiveness, or a group ideology of working for the nation. Some people can come up with creative solutions, and do well for themselves. The thing that makes this feasible, is only if individuals don't feel constrained from the freedom to pollute more, but feel engaged in the attempt to succeed and make progress in a world where not caring about pollution is to not care about other people, which is inhumane.

The many methods of accounting for the quantities of carbon produced by each person, or each country, such as cap and trade, all have their ups and downs. The credibility of any of these working though, is psychological. If there is no basic acknowledgment that we are in trouble, we will not activate the creative and resourceful parts of our minds at working around this bump in the road. Technological solutions and socio-economic conditions can easily be put in place, unless this is going to make the herd grumpy. For this reason, it is the will of the current individualist consumers which is keeping the path unsustainable. With a psychological change of one salient feature, allowing a new variable into judgements, this whole steering group of momentum can point motivation into the direction of a world which can keep changing, but in a way which doesn't stamp on itself without acknowledging this accidental pain. There can be a shift in general understanding, making things operate roughly the same as they did wherever you are, apart from the new variable being factored in.

This small change in thinking, does though make a huge difference in the psychological relationship between humans and the world, in the mindset of individuals. This could be described as a change in disposition relevant to humans as a species. Compared to divine command, or fatalism, having a pattern of recognition of the interactiveness of human behaviour and the state of the planet is relatively simple and materialistic, but far from the basic animalistic 'desire and attain' motivational programme of action, which is short-sighted in both space and time.

As instability of food supplies increase, this will not be followed by passive realignment of populations. Borders and boundaries are already there, as are collective, regional identities. For the West to maintain its' high standard of living, resources from other regions are needed. Hospitality for people from all over the world who wish to have this life-style is not going to be an open door policy. There is a limit to how much blame and responsibility can be used as justificatory measures to explain the changing world as the drawbridge literally comes up as borders tighten, in a country which has a social mindset stuck in the status quo. This strategy of an unchanging paradigm, has after effects on the frame of thinking, requiring new modifications and maintenance in explaining its' adequacy. This is an important hinge point, as the state of the mind of people who have freshened up their programme of assessment to change, as the world and our understanding of it does, differs widely from those who do not. This can be at the personal and cultural level. In how we frame the surrounding events is personal. But it turns out, the majority rule of this headspace, actually determines the future in how that will be brought about by a culture and society that thinks in those terms of understanding. The modus operandi can continue on the same path, which as circumstance deepens, will bring with it feedback onto the psychological pattern with which it frames the surrounding trauma. This at its' most severe, will be moving the goalposts of morality. Responsibility and blame will become increasingly diverted with fictitious knowledge, or the principles of consideration will have to be adapted to suit the new circumstances.

As displacement of people increases, including from violent actions which normally follow survival instability, borders will tighten. In a world two degrees hotter, humans aren't about to develop an unprecedented collective compassion of understanding. The discussion here, is about the acceptance of the need to take seriously the need to reduce pollution. This will not stop the trouble in its' tracks. But this is a psychological acceptance of responsibility. The opposite of this is the idea of how to describe the background with which to frame the mind trying to justify the walls going up around the consumerist culture, in order to keep the suffering out.

We have highlighted the expected responses from individuals' type-cast paradigms. The main tide of a cultural mind-set which judges these, is more set on the aspirations of the future goals than a dissection of existing personal psychological triggers. This is a 'where are we going', or trying to go, collective ideology, which may or may not, find delusional mindsets tolerable, or even preferable. This question of cultural identity, is the one which will define the pace at which flatearthers become identifiable as daft, versus being blended in as a minority mind-set, entitled to their beliefs. As there are costs, in either effort, attention or money, in curtailing pollution, the ability of people to not care based on a fictional version of reality, is a tell-tale sign of the state of the culture and its' version of what it thinks it is heading towards. This is not a deliberate disregard for any consequential damage, purely a guiding light of generality, which may or may not shine on this or that aspect of existence.

Aspirations, as much as the existing nuts and bolts, are what guide paradigms into what they interpret reality as being. Our methods of compatmentalizing all the elements which make up the judgments of our interactive effectiveness with the world we make, have feedback effects on how we think the world is. The way we interpret our surroundings, can be generated by our thoughts on what we think we are part of. The sorts of material possessions we are used to seeing, what we consider normal activities, and which of these things are judged as desirable or admirable, are major features of how we frame our thinking on where we are, and where we wish to be within that scenario. This is not a breaking down of evidence and an analysis of forecasted outcomes, it is based on hopes and desires. The things we wish to be or have, need to be attained in a process we can see as being feasible in the world in front of us without any revolutionary innovation. In this way, the means to that end, are what our culture or society has placed in an accessible toolbox. If we use these things according to the configuration they are designed for, we all vary in what makes us. But these many little or big differences all make little divergence when compared to the general centre-point mark of what our cultural identity shows we are geared towards. Any of us can spot the general direction a herd of lots of individualists are heading in. This is why when addressing the issue, the concept of adaptation tends to look at those suffering needing to change. This is not a reflective tactic of seeing how our own systems need to be adapted to not cause the trouble.

Depressive observers is a fantastically pessimistic stereotype of those people with the closest connection to reality. This unfortunate typecast have a good ability to forecast without egocentric rigging of the bets, but will hopefully become outnumbered by a populous of people capable of acknowledging this, without a sense of despair. It should be with a sense of accomplishment that anyone is willing to take this standpoint, at the price of the understanding that things are going wrong. To remain cheerful whilst accepting difficulties, may take some mental effort, but less so the more popular it is, as the language of acceptance will not be as misunderstood or rejected as it currently is. There is a kind of bravery in taking stock of the far from ideal state of play, which would hopefully lead to more of a recognition of realism than negativity. The point of being a realist, is to make efforts in the direction of avoiding bad things happening, not to create doom out of a mindscape.

Taking the blinkers off is to be aware of something and respond to it, not to hinder progress. This can be contrasted to the effort needed to remain convinced that reality is not in this situation, in a world which is getting hotter, quite fast, at a rate that as yet, has still not been slowed by collaborative global efforts. Over the next few decades, patterns of movement of foodstuffs and people will be shifting. Even animals will migrate to places they didn't used to go before. Weather patterns and the amount of ice on the surface are changing, in ways which can be measured. As a society, we are a long way from this being accepted without knee jerking this doom away with many emotionally triggered responses. So what would be enough for more people to take reality on the chin like depressive observers? Unfortunately it is obvious why this is not a naturally attractive standpoint. However, it should be a known psychological feature that we live in a state of flexibility in terms of identity. So having a basic adherence to the principles of reducing pollution, doesn't make the individual steadfast on this mind-set permanently. Depending on social or physical situations we all bend a bit. This makes the depressive observers a bad analogy, as they are stuck, maybe only temporarily, in a state of being which makes the future more open to unbiased speculation than consumer based idealists. Most of our flexible identities can make analytic and considerate moral deliberations, until Friday, when we can't sit still. Realism doesn't have to be taken as a bitter pill that will remove the possibility of ever being a short-sighted, selfish consumer of candy-flavoured tripe.

Two approaches of attitude which do not start with responsibility, are feasible to frame the situation of migration barriers coinciding with the unsustainable changes in temperature. To blame the situation on others outside of your own countries borders, is a simple strategy of diverting responsibility, in a very comprehensible and close to reality format. This can also take some of the responsibility, in a calibrating fashion, where one's own country is a small piece of a very big causal situation, and can be seen as having had very little control over the outcome of the big picture. In other words diminished responsibility. The second, more severe stance to justify the geographical bias to access of well-being, is to define the physical barrier to moral concern to the limits of national identity. This is a quite likely, and pitiful reverse of human development. Having the need to back-pedal from a mature level of consideration, due to an accidental balls-up of our own, but mostly in other peoples' surroundings, is literally going backwards and is shameful.

The 'putting yourself first' strategy for a nation, when under pressure from foreign populations is very simple to suggest and enforce. This is due to the understanding that the alternative paradigm is to put yourself second. A country should make sure things are Ok for itself before doing work on the welfare of people outside its' borders. The reason this is so easy to get the majority to take on board as a primary driver, is that the opposed idea is that this would need to be reversed by analysing the state of the world first, before looking at issues closer to home. This is not naturally credible for a herd of consumers, or most normal people with a natural amount of self-interest. Damage is being done to world beyond borders due to activity now. When the circumstance shows difficulties elsewhere in the future, this suffering can be left out there as well. Messing up other peoples survival by not caring about anything that is not in your own countries boundaries, does bring an obvious ethical naivety, which cannot be justified by the 'put yourself first' principle; which is in its' simple form a decision strategy over where *priorities* lie, not a demarcation over what matters and what never does. This is why when the borders are tightened, there will be a kind of 'we do care, but..' justificatory epilogue.

The need to express concern is there in our general moral make-up, but can be purposely constrained by describing how the situation makes this consideration not available, not through a willingness to tolerate suffering, but as a result of putting things in a simple order of what to do first. This is an almost inevitable follow up to climate change, of societal, psychological frameworks with which to cope with changing pressures, on those most likely to have caused the difficulties. The declaration of not having meant to cause this, along with a natural ability to care, is still real. But this is not going to shift the history of who caused the most pollution, nor move priorities away from westernised consumers wanting to have as many comforts as they can have access to.

This difficult but not unrealistic forecast is a bit simple, in being a pattern of crop failures, food shortages and mass migration from 'have not' to 'have' territories. There may be a softer transition, where some areas become less inhabitable, and over time people leave these areas and adapt to different locations and cultures, with only a small amount of loss of life. Also, there will be some difficulties in well populated, wealthy, westernised consumer based societies, which are in for changes including flooding of cities and drought effecting both agricultural and domestic use of water. This has been investigated by some NGO's, showing how the ability to adapt, is to some extent based upon the wealth of those suffering. This differs from the *most at risk*. When situations globally are more complicated than a simple pattern of analysis of transition, the psychological formulas with which to categorize information can be proxies. Warfare and disruption make changes in weather patterns seem hardly relevant, even if these are the factors with the greatest inertia. The field of vision narrows morally for everyday use, rather than dissect and categorise different dilemmas. This is where an individual doesn't make the 'do or don't care' decision. There is a generalisation of being in a relatively easy position compared to those in great difficulties, and taking a recognition of some of the history of pollution caused so far, but in a defensive home-ground of not being capable of changing the mix of suffering beyond the borders. The great divide described earlier, was between either accepting the difficulties of pollution and allowing this to affect activities, or remaining in denial by transferring responsibility or narrowing morality.

Even if the holy grail of adaptive measures are taken, there will still be a transition into a differently organised planet. The will to reduce pollution now, will not reverse a lot of the changes that are on their way. For this reason, the boundaries of consideration are still going to be on a psychological platform, which is going to be stressed, stretched or changed. The way that responsibility for the past is labelled, can vary along a sliding rule of application. The situation can be blamed on other countries, followed by the need, or not, to respond, regardless of the location of its' cause. An alternative is to add a level of own nation blameworthiness, from a little to a lot, again followed by the need to respond regardless of cause. Third is the denial of blame within any western society. All of these views are justificatory measures for the unpleasant but deemed necessary jingoism.

The state of the Western nations' cultural identity, in terms of planetary responsibility, are currently in what is left of being in good shape, and moderately coping with strains of a global economic fumble. Our view of ourselves in the West, is largely positive, and is not on the whole, that made of people who consider their culture to be inconsiderate or harmful. Productive, developed, high-tech and democratic are more the general ethos. How this can adapt to the request for an increasingly rigid demarcation between those outside of the nations borders and those within, depends upon a story of circumstance, with a change to moral identity. What this story is depends more on the need for a result than on what has happened.

Having a description of the history of change that has brought about the need for walls around the life-style of the West, would, without stretching the truth, have references to an inability to reduce pollution in time to prevent the fast warming of the planet. This would however, not be accompanied by a new high standard of living provided without pollution being caused, at least not for a long transition period of development of barriers and technology. How to cope psychologically, with the limited-access-benefits of the poison of history, puts desire onto any open avenue for alleviating the hypercritical consumerist posture. The herd are walking into a very difficult dead-end, where happiness is only feasible if the suffering of people outside of geographical boundaries is not a hindrance. How this can be woken up to, when the general sense of identity is that of a nation seeing itself as a progressive, westernised democracy makes an uneasy about-turn situation. There is a difficulty in the identity of self and other. The general understanding in the West is that we have already developed, which brings with it a resulting approximation that those outside our borders are not so developed or progressed. This paradigm of having what others do not, due to their not having done so well in some aspects of living, apportions blame and pity outwardly. If this is accompanied by greater difficulties and suffering of these nations, made by our own productivity systems, this is hard to shoe-horn into the 'self-worth, others needy' mindset. Circumstance is usually a mixed bag, as in 'it is not all our fault that this, but a bit of that', but psychologically, we tend to sweep things into a one sided bag. For that reason, the consumerist individualist, is not about to lose faith in the market economy or materialist goals above all else. Either morality will tighten or blame will remain facing outward. The reality is that the West has made many great leaps forward, and developed, but with some bits not being positive. A calculated response to this, is that we can look at the ranges of development, admit to the damage done in some areas, and work on a new path forward from there. Unfortunately this is not nearly as available psychologically as it is on paper as a formula. Good or bad, like black or white, binary readings, are how we frame our national identity when negotiating deals on how to approach the future. The idea of splitting this into segments, and recognizing our accidental damage in parts of this, is effective as a negotiator format, when compromise is never far away, but is not how a culture moves its' headspace.

The consumerist ideology has taken such a good hold on societies cultural perspective, that morality is already in the general state of inactivity compared with self-interest and gratification - meaning further steps of delusional justifications, or unconscious forms of repressed feelings, will find the future easy pickings. Squabbling is a more likely form of global discussion, than rational deliberation. This is a question of identity, as the negotiation of how to deal with large scale changes involving blame, responsibility and adaptation, need to be between the societies they represent, which need a collective understanding of involvement, this being at the opposite end of the scale to the current individualism. Half-asleep and wearing a badge of progressive self-interest, the herd want the gates to their playground to be kept safely shut, with or without any knowledge of what is on the outside of it. This is not a description of a suggested policy change to a world without borders. What can be seen, is that there is a natural progression of where we are now, to somewhere worse, coming from the cultural, societal, psychological, paradigms we have become stuck to. These things are not fixed though through necessity, and changes can come which are attractive when tallied with reality. The variations of response being that they can be ignored, twisted or more positively, assessed and updated.

The interesting phenomena to comprehend, is the fineness of the line that is determining the flavour of the future in developed western consumer societies. The ideas of competition and self-interest can remain intact. The free-market can operate unimpeded in order to deliver goods and services most efficiently. The society enjoying the benefits of this can feel a connectedness with the entire world, without raising a moral code-of-interest barrier of 'us and them'. If all the things we buy, want and consume are competing, not just for cost reduction and profit-making, but to impress their consumers that the way they provide this, causes less pollution and damage to the world than their competitors do, the future is the same, just not screwed up. Psychologically, this does not bring about a new-found need for twisting the truth or repressing consideration. Even when economically part through a collapse of global security, there is a general understanding of self-identity of most nations being on the fix-it side of the suffering. The sooner a society accepts involvement, the less stressful, psychologically, is the transition the world makes in front of us. A bit like living a lie, the longer we drag out disbelief in the need for change, the more humiliating the about-turn becomes. So much so that it is quite common to have an unconscious desire to pass on all the shame to future generations, whilst wearing a luxuriously expensive mask of ignorance.

Printed in Great Britain
by Amazon